PEARL HARBOR

Roosevelt and the Coming of the War

Problems in American Civilization

UNDER THE EDITORIAL DIRECTION OF

George Rogers Taylor

PEARL HARBOR
Roosevelt and the Coming of the War

EDITED WITH AN INTRODUCTION BY
George M. Waller

Problems in American Civilization

READINGS SELECTED BY THE
DEPARTMENT OF AMERICAN STUDIES
AMHERST COLLEGE

D. C. HEATH AND COMPANY: Boston

INTRODUCTION

IN Teheran and Tokyo, in Rio de Janeiro and Ottawa, in Paris and London — in every capital city around the world the eyes of political leaders are focused on Washington. The position of the United States has become so important that even a threatened shift in American foreign policy may precipitate in one country or another a fiscal crisis, the fall of a government, or the inauguration of revolution. With world power has come world responsibility. American foreign policy, long little more than a by-product of domestic issues, is now, in the middle of the twentieth century, a central factor in the economics and politics of a considerable part of the world.

Foreign policy is determined in totalitarian countries by a few leaders whose word is law. In democratic countries it is formed in an atmosphere of free discussion and debate by officials responsible ultimately to the voting public. So in this country when issues of foreign policy have risen to the fore a full dress debate has ensued, a debate which reflects the interests involved, the interests of economic groups who see most clearly their own advantage and all too often identify it with the general good, the interests of foreign immigrant groups who have not forgotten Old World wrongs or loyalties, the interests of political parties and leaders who sometimes confuse national interest with partisan advantage. Even those with wide vision who seem most able to free themselves from personal or partisan

considerations, statesmen, scholars, public leaders, and plain, conscientious citizens, have divided into divergent groups, some sincerely believing in a strictly nationalistic or isolationist approach and others urging a world-wide view of the problem.

So it was that the United States, during the era of the French Revolution and the Napoleonic Wars, was sharply divided between sympathizers with the erstwhile mother country and those who sided with France, our Revolutionary ally. The War of 1812 was preceded by long debate in government and out, for and against the ambitions of the War Hawks. Problems of continental expansion involved lengthy disputes and political partisanship in connection with the Louisiana Purchase, the acquisition of Florida, Texas annexation, the war with Mexico, and the acquisition of territory along the northern boundary in Maine and Oregon. Even the Monroe Doctrine, as generally accepted as it came to be, was sometimes passed over in silence, sometimes invoked, and sometimes extended beyond its original meaning, depending on the viewpoints of changing administrations.

On the eve of every major war it has been characteristic of Americans to engage in a "great debate" over involvement in it and to close ranks and present a united front once the decision to fight has been made. But once the war is over, historians, political leaders, and others have been wont to reopen the debate, reviewing the causes of war in the light of historical hindsight and revising judgments previously made concerning the issues, the necessity for war, war guilt, and the nature of the peace settlement. This "revisionism" reflects in part the attempt of students of history to put the past crisis in perspective in the period following the emotional stresses and strains of actual warfare. It also arises from the re-emergence of partisan differences which were largely submerged during the war. And, finally, it reflects a deep and disturbing divergence among citizens on the proper role of America in world affairs.

The readings in this volume are focused on the entrance of the United States into World War II. How and why was our decision made to enter that conflict? Was President Franklin D. Roosevelt personally responsible for plunging us into an unnecessary war? Could the United States wisely have avoided war by pursuing a different policy? And what would have been the chief characteristics of such a policy?

The arguments having to do with these questions are compounded of various beliefs and allegations, sometimes even mutually contradictory. Roosevelt's detractors are represented in the following readings by men like Charles A. Beard, the "sage of New Milford," Connecticut, eminent historian, a past president of the American Historical Association, and one-time professor at Columbia University. Another is William Henry Chamberlin, well-known author and lecturer, editorial writer for the *Wall Street Journal* and for over ten years Moscow correspondent for the *Christian Science Monitor*. These men charge the President and his advisers with leading the country into war while professing a policy of peace. The evidence suggests to them that even while he iterated "again and again and again" his pol-

icy of avoiding war, Roosevelt was irrevocably committing America to the cause of the anti-Axis powers, knowing that "all aid short of war" would not be enough. When he found isolationist opposition too strong to enable him to bring the United States into the war on the side of Britain, they charge that he turned to the Far East and "maneuvered" Japan into striking the blow which would accomplish his purpose. "He lied the American people into war because he could not lead them into it," were the pungent words of Clare Boothe Luce.

One group of the President's supporters goes a considerable distance toward admitting this charge. A foremost student of American diplomacy, Thomas A. Bailey, has said,

Because the masses are notoriously short-sighted and generally cannot see the danger until it is at their throats our statesmen are forced to deceive them into an awareness of their own long run interests. This is clearly what Roosevelt had to do, and who shall say that posterity will not thank him for it?[1]

Among the proponents of the Administration, Herbert Feis, an economist and a member of the policy-planning staff of the State Department, is represented in these readings. He, along with Robert Sherwood and historian Arthur M. Schlesinger, Jr., agrees substantially with Bailey, finding extenuation in the short-sighted opposition of the isolationists who were ready to block measures deemed essential to the country's security.

The readings present others, like Basil Rauch, professor of history at Columbia, who, with Dexter Perkins, William L. Langer, and S. E. Gleason, support Roosevelt, maintaining that he had no desire to lead the United States into war. The Presi-

[1] *The Man in the Street* (New York, 1948), p. 13.

dent's statements, they hold, were designed to inform the people of the growing crisis and win their support for a policy of active participation in measures of collective security, the only course open to a nation professing adherence to principles of morality and international law. If the policy of "internationalism" failed to avoid war it was because the course of the totalitarian powers finally left no alternative to war. They steadfastly affirm that Roosevelt took all possible measures to keep America out of war short of shamefully abandoning American principles and exposing the nation to extreme peril. They credit him with gaining time for preparedness and place the blame for delays in the build-up of American armed strength on isolationist obstruction which prevented early and adequate application of measures of collective security while such measures might have had a chance for success.

Such obstructionism, they maintain, deprived American outposts of men and material and resulted in the inability of the outposts to ward off the Japanese attack. Nevertheless, according to this view, the outpost commanders were derelict in being caught unawares. On this latter point Roosevelt's critics aver that since the Administration was consciously maneuvering Japan into the war it was an act of criminal negligence not to keep the outposts better informed about the developing crisis. They shift the blame for the disaster at Pearl Harbor as well as for the coming of the war to their main target, Roosevelt.

Such writers as Frederick C. Sanborn, an international law expert, Harry Elmer Barnes, historian and sociologist, John T. Flynn, and Charles C. Tansill charge that the Administration turned to war to cover up its failures in domestic politics. Roosevelt wanted to insure his own re-election

and even had grandiose ideas of world leadership, according to these writers. They were heartened by the testimony of Jesse Jones, Secretary of Commerce under Roosevelt, who noted,

One serious problem with Mr. Roosevelt after the start of World War II in 1939 was that he was always fighting two wars at the same time, the political struggle for the Presidency, which he never lost sight of, and the military conflict. Regardless of his oft repeated statement, "I hate war," he was eager to get into the fighting since that would insure a third term.[2]

A major issue emerging from the controversy concerns the conflicting judgments on the nature of the war. This issue is represented in the reading by the selection from Charles C. Tansill, professor of diplomatic history at Georgetown University and author of one of the important revisionist works on the causes of America's entry into World War II. Tansill builds a case to show that the United States misunderstood the problem facing the Japanese. He, along with other students of American foreign policy like A. Whitney Griswold and George F. Kennan, believes that Japan saw more clearly than the United States the probability that Russian influence would become dominant over a decadent China if Japan withdrew. The persistent myth that American interests were more closely identified with China than with Japan blinded the United States to the realities of Far Eastern politics. We sided with China against Japan whereas the latter was in actuality the more logical object of our support, whether as customer or as ally in the struggle against Communistic totalitarianism. By our own past actions we had alienated Japan and forced her to look for support to the Axis.

[2] *Fifty Billion Dollars* (New York, 1951), p. 260.

But where Kennan and Griswold conclude that Roosevelt and Hull bent their best efforts to re-establishing good relations with Japan, albeit rather too late, Tansill, with Beard, Chamberlin, Barnes, George Morgenstern, and others of Roosevelt's critics, maintains that the Administration rejected sincere Japanese proposals for peace and refused to take into account the serious problems Japan faced in the Far East. Japan, according to these writers, was eager to abandon its expansionist program in Asia and wanted only time and a chance to save face.

For these critics the situation faced by the United States in these postwar years is evidence that the war should have been avoided. It destroyed the alignment of powers and left the country worse off than before. They deny, in fact, that the struggles in Europe and Asia were a threat to American security. Judged by the diplomacy which followed in the war years and the postwar era, intervention in the name of international law or moral principles strikes them as hypocritical or unrealistic.

Roosevelt's adherents find this wisdom of hindsight insufficient to condemn Roosevelt and his advisers for action taken on the basis of the best analysis then available. They charge their opponents with distorting the picture as it really was, ignoring the threat of totalitarianism on the Right which was as great as the shadow of Communism on the Left. Much as Hull may have been concerned with finding an answer to Japan's problems, he could not condone actions contrary to American principles, nor could he forget Japan's attachment to the Axis powers, who were, in the opinion of the Administration and contrary to the stand of the isolationists, a serious menace to the future of the United States. Japanese expansion threatened the exposed holdings of the anti-Axis powers who could not afford to divert strength from the struggle in Western Europe. Since, in this view, the fight being waged against the Axis was our fight, Japan's policy had to be opposed, even at the risk of war.

The foregoing summary provides merely an introduction to the debate which the student will find in the following pages. It is a dispute which will be a continuing one, not because many facts are still in doubt (although as time goes on some important new evidence may be revealed), but chiefly because persons with varying interests and philosophies interpret the facts in different ways and come to divergent conclusions. The student today who will share with his fellow citizens the responsibility of determining foreign policy in the years immediately ahead, though he read this volume with considerable care, cannot expect to emerge with easy or simple answers. Like his elders of 1938–1941 he will have to develop his own attitude and find his own answers as the problems arise. For that student, then, this volume is prepared in the belief that through the thoughtful study of this "great debate" he may be better prepared to play his part in the continuing international crisis of our time.

[NOTE: The statements in "The Clash of Issues" on page xiii are from the following sources: William Henry Chamberlin: *America's Second Crusade,* pages 130–131, 147; Harry Elmer Barnes: *The Struggle against the Historical Blackout;* George Morgenstern: *Pearl Harbor: The Story of the Secret War* (New York, 1947), page 329; Forrest Davis and Ernest K. Lindley: *How War Came* (New York, 1942), page 203; Joseph W. Ballantine: "Mukden to Pearl Harbor," *Foreign Affairs* (July, 1949), page 664.]

CONTENTS

CHRONOLOGY

1927	Japan invades Manchuria
1931	Hoover's Secretary of State announces the *Stimson Doctrine*
1933	Japan leaves the League of Nations
1935	Italy attacks Ethiopia
1936	Spanish Civil War; Germany reoccupies the Rhineland
1937	Japan opens undeclared war on China
1935–37	U. S. passes Neutrality Acts
1937	Roosevelt's *Quarantine Speech*
1938	Hitler takes Austria; British and French sign the *Munich Pact* "appeasing" Hitler
March, 1939	Hitler takes Czechoslovakia; Mussolini invades Albania
July, 1939	U.S. gives Japan notice of abrogation of reciprocal trade treaties
August, 1939	Germany and Russia sign nonaggression pact
September 3, 1939	WAR: Hitler invades Poland; Britain and France declare war on Germany
November, 1939	U. S. Congress repeals arms embargo, puts trade with belligerents on "cash and carry" basis
April–June, 1940	*Blitzkrieg:* Fall of Denmark, Norway, The Netherlands, Belgium, France
September, 1940	Destroyer-Bases Agreement
September, 1940	Congress passes Selective Service Act, by one-vote margin
November, 1940	Roosevelt re-elected for third term
January–March, 1941	Joint military staff talks, U. S. and Britain
March, 1941	Lend-Lease Act
March, 1941	Hull and Nomura begin talks in Washington
April, 1941	Roosevelt orders U. S. Navy to patrol in Western Atlantic
June, 1941	Hitler attacks Russia
July, 1941	U. S. occupies Iceland bases
July, 1941	Japanese Imperial Conference determines to continue policy in Asia
July 24, 1941	Japan moves into Indo-China
July 26, 1941	U. S. freezes Japanese assets
August 9–14, 1941	Atlantic Conference: Roosevelt and Churchill meet at Argentia
August 17, 1941	U. S. warning to Japan
August–September, 1941	Prime Minister Konoye requests meeting with Roosevelt
September–October, 1941	U. S. destroyers attacked in Atlantic
September 6, 1941	Konoye offers proposals to U. S.
October 2, 1941	U. S. note rejecting Konoye's proposals and deferring proposed meeting
October 17, 1941	Konoye Cabinet falls; Tojo becomes Prime Minister
November 7, 1941	U. S. rejects Japanese Imperial Conference's "Proposal A"
November 17, 1941	Kurusu arrives in Washington to join Nomura
November 20, 1941	U. S. rejects Japanese "Proposal B"

THE CLASH OF ISSUES

Roosevelt's opponents maintain:

... America was stealthily maneuvered into war behind the backs
and without the knowledge of the elected representatives of the
American people.... Like the Roman god Janus, Roosevelt in the
prewar period had two faces. For the American people, for the
public record, there was the face of bland assurance that his first
concern was to keep the country out of war. But in more intimate
surroundings the Chief Executive often assumed that America
was already involved in war.... Seldom if ever in American history was there such a gulf between appearances and realities,
between Presidential words and Presidential deeds.

WILLIAM HENRY CHAMBERLIN

... Roosevelt and Hull knew from the cracked Japanese code that
the Japanese peace offers were sincere and reasonable, but, nevertheless, rebuffed them and provoked the Japanese attack on Pearl
Harbor.

HARRY ELMER BARNES

... no amount of excuses will palliate the conduct of President
Roosevelt and his advisers. The offense of which they stand con-
victed is not failure to discharge their responsibilities, but calculated refusal to do so. They failed — with calculation — to keep
the United States out of war and to avoid a clash with Japan....
The "warnings" they sent to Hawaii failed — and were so phrased
and so handled as to insure failure.

GEORGE MORGENSTERN

*Roosevelt himself sought methods short of war by which the
nation's security could be safeguarded:*

If Great Britain goes down, the Axis powers will control the continents of Europe, Asia, Africa, Australia and the high seas — and
they will be in a position to bring enormous military and naval
resources against this hemisphere.... There is far less chance of
the United States getting into the war if we do all we can now to
support the nations defending themselves against the Axis....

Fireside Chat, December 29, 1940

His supporters conclude:

On the American side the perspective is unclouded. This government hoped, against its better judgment, for a comprehensive
settlement of the Far Eastern problems, and, failing that, nursed

a more limited and pragmatic hope that hostilities might be staved
off for as long as the Japanese were willing to talk.

FORREST DAVIS and ERNEST K. LINDLEY

And a State Department expert on the Far East writes:

The Japanese were not offering to negotiate a reasonable settlement by processes of agreement; they were presenting demands,
to be accepted or rejected. The United States had only two
choices: either to yield to the Japanese demands and sacrifice
principles and security, or to decline to yield and take the
consequences.

JOSEPH W. BALLANTINE

William Henry Chamberlin:

ROOSEVELT MANEUVERS
AMERICA INTO WAR

THE momentous issue of deliberate involvement in the European war might well have been submitted to a referendum of the American people in the presidential election of 1940. The majority of the Republicans in both houses of Congress before and after this election systematically voted against measures calculated to bring about this involvement.

Had Roosevelt frankly presented to the voters the program which he actually carried out in 1941 (lend-lease, convoys, undeclared shooting war in the Atlantic, commercial blockade of Japan) and had Roosevelt's opponent been a sincerely noninterventionist Republican a very interesting discussion would certainly have ensued. The verdict of the people would then have given a clear mandate either to go into the war frankly and vigorously or to stay out of it, except in the event of direct attack.

But neither of the leading candidates in the 1940 election made a candid statement of his position on the most important issue confronting the American people. A comparison of Roosevelt's words before the election and of his deeds after the election fully substantiates the tart comment of Clare Boothe Luce: "He lied the American people into war because he could not lead them into it."

And by an unfortunate accident of American politics the Republican nomination did not go to a man who shared the viewpoint of the majority of Republican members of Congress. The candidate was Wendell Willkie, a newcomer in politics, a man who in the preceding autumn had volunteered to raise money for interventionist purposes.

The result was that the very large number of American voters who wanted to stay out of the war were, for all practical purposes, disfranchised. The campaign was an amazing exhibition of double talk. Roosevelt and Willkie vied with each other in making the most sweeping promises to keep the country at peace. The frequency and forcefulness of these pledges mounted to a crescendo as the election day approached. This was a significant straw in the wind, indicating how the majority of voters in both parties felt on the issue. There were evidently few votes to be won and many to be lost by a frank call to arms.

Both platforms contained antiwar commitments. The Democratic read: "We will not participate in foreign wars and we will not send our army, naval or air forces to fight in foreign lands outside the Americas, except in case of attack."

The equivalent Republican statement was more concise: "The Republican Party is firmly opposed to involving this nation in foreign wars."

Willkie said in Chicago on September 13: "If you elect me President, I will never send an American boy to fight in a European war."

From *America's Second Crusade* by William Henry Chamberlin (Chicago: Henry Regnery Company), excerpted material from pages 120–147. Reprinted by permission.

He told his audience in Cleveland on October 2: "I am for keeping out of war. I am for peace for America."

He declared in Philadelphia on October 4: "We must stop this drift toward war," and in a radio broadcast on October 8 he asserted: "We must keep out of war at all hazards." He told the voters of Boston on October 11: "Our boys shall stay out of European wars." On October 22 he offered the following explanation of the difference between his foreign policy and that of the Administration:

"One difference is my determination to stay out of war. I have a real fear that this Administration is heading for war, and I am against our going to war and will do all that I can to avoid it."

So Willkie, whose whole attitude after the election promoted the "drift toward war" which he condemned before the votes were counted, tried to win as the champion of peace against war. But he could not outbid Roosevelt in promises on this issue. Between October 28 and November 3 the President gave repeated assurances that he would not lead the country into any foreign wars. As his admirer, Robert E. Sherwood, says:

That Madison Square Garden speech (on October 28) was one of the most equivocal of Roosevelt's career. . . . Here Roosevelt went to the length or depth of taking credit for the Neutrality Law and other measures which he had thoroughly disapproved and had fought to repeal and had contrived by all possible means to circumvent. While boasting of the Neutrality Law as part of the Administration record, he deliberately neglected to make any mention of his own Quarantine Speech.[1]

Two days later, in Boston, Roosevelt went even further. "Fear-of-war hysteria,"

in Sherwood's phrase, seemed to be growing. Telegrams poured in from Democratic leaders, urging the President to make stronger and more specific antiwar pledges. The election, according to these telegrams, hung in the balance. Henri IV thought Paris was worth a Mass. Roosevelt apparently believed that another term of power was worth promises which would soon be disregarded, which could be broken without incurring legal liability. At the urging of Sherwood[2] he decided to strengthen his pledge with the words "again and again and again." And the rich, soothing voice poured out to the audience at Boston the following reassurance:

While I am talking to you, mothers and fathers, I give you one more assurance.

I have said this before, but I shall say it again and again and again.

Your boys are not going to be sent into any foreign wars.

On November 2 Roosevelt promised: "Your President says this nation is not going to war."

On November 3 he added: "The first purpose of our foreign policy is to keep our country out of war."[3]

No isolationist could have offered more sweeping and categorical pledges. How these pledges were observed will be the subject of the next two chapters. Professor Thomas A. Bailey, a sympathizer with Roosevelt's foreign policy, admits that the President's tactics were disingenuous, but offers an apology in the following passage:

Franklin Roosevelt repeatedly deceived the

[1] *Roosevelt and Hopkins* (New York, Harper, 1948), p. 189.

[2] *Ibid.*, p. 191.
[3] For a complete survey of the antiwar professions of Roosevelt and Willkie, see Charles A. Beard, *American Foreign Policy, 1932–1940* (Yale University Press, 1946), pp. 265–323.

American people during the period before Pearl Harbor. . . . He was like the physician who must tell the patient lies for the patient's own good. . . . The country was overwhelmingly non-interventionist to the very day of Pearl Harbor, and an overt attempt to lead the people into war would have resulted in certain failure and an almost certain ousting of Roosevelt in 1940, with a consequent defeat of his ultimate aims.[4]

Professor Bailey offers the following somewhat Machiavellian conception as to how democracy should work.

A president who cannot entrust the people with the truth betrays a certain lack of faith in the basic tenets of democracy. But because the masses are notoriously shortsighted and generally cannot see danger until it is at their throats our statesmen are forced to deceive them into an awareness of their own long run interests. This is clearly what Roosevelt had to do, and who shall say that posterity will not thank him for it?

That Roosevelt resorted to habitual deception of the American people both before and after the election of 1940 is not open to serious question. That such deception, on an issue which was literally a matter of life and death for many American citizens, savors of personal dictatorship rather than of democracy, responsive to the popular will, also seems obvious.

Whether Roosevelt's deception was justified is open to debate. This is a question which everyone must answer on the basis of what America's Second Crusade cost, what it accomplished, what kind of world emerged from it, and how real was the danger against which it was undertaken.

Road to War: The Atlantic

Roosevelt was elected President for a third term by the votes of isolationists

[4] Thomas A. Bailey, *The Man in the Street* (New York, Macmillan, 1948), pp. 11–13.

who trusted his dozen or more specific pledges to stay out of war and of interventionists who did not believe he meant what he said. The latter had far more reason for satisfaction. Once assured of four more years in the White House, Roosevelt set the ship of state on a much more militant course. But the double talk, the carrying out of steps which logically pointed to full belligerence to an accompaniment of soothing "no war" assurances, continued almost until Pearl Harbor . . .

Immediately after the election there was a political lull. Roosevelt departed on December 2 on a Caribbean cruise with Harry Hopkins as his only guest. The President was apparently mainly concerned with rest and recreation. But on this cruise he received a very important letter from Winston Churchill. In this communication, dated December 8, one finds the final inspiration for the lend-lease idea.

Churchill emphasized two points: the serious threat of the submarine war and the approaching exhaustion of Britain's financial assets. He suggested that America should protect its shipments to Britain with warships. Realizing that this was probably too much to expect, he suggested, as an alternative, "the gift, loan or supply of a large number of American vessels of war." Another proposal, which was soon to bear fruit, was that the United States Navy should "extend its sea control of the American side of the Atlantic."

Churchill warned that the moment was approaching "when we shall no longer be able to pay cash for shipping and other supplies." After receiving this letter Roosevelt, according to Hopkins, came out one evening with the whole lend-lease scheme, the delivery of munitions and supplies free of charge to Great Britain and the other anti-Axis belligerents.

"He didn't seem to have any clear idea how it could be done legally," Hopkins observes. "But there wasn't a doubt in his mind that he would find a way to do it."

After returning to Washington Roosevelt outlined the principle of lend-lease at a press conference. He used as an illustration the case of a man lending his garden hose to a neighbor whose house was on fire.

In the course of his "fireside" chat to the American people on December 29 the President painted a dire picture of the peril that was supposedly hanging over the Western Hemisphere.

Never since Jamestown and Plymouth Rock has American civilization been in such danger as now. . . . If Great Britain goes down, the Axis powers will control the continents of Europe, Asia, Africa, Australia and the high seas — and they will be in a position to bring enormous military and naval resources against this hemisphere. It is no exaggeration to say that all of us in the Americas would be living at the point of a gun — a gun loaded with explosive bullets, economic as well as military.

Yet along with this melodramatic scare note, which was to be struck again and again during 1941, there were soothing assurances that the United States would not get into the war.

There is far less chance of the United States getting into the war if we do all we can now to support the nations defending themselves against the Axis. . . . You can therefore nail any talk about sending armies to Europe as deliberate untruth. . . . We must be the arsenal of democracy.

Roosevelt outlined the plan for lend-lease aid to the anti-Axis powers in his message to Congress of January 6, 1941. This was the longest single stride on the road to war. For it is a long-recognized principle of international law that it is an act of war for a neutral government (as distinguished from private firms or agencies) to supply arms, munitions, and implements of war to a belligerent.

The United States had demanded and obtained heavy damages, by decision of a court of arbitration, from Great Britain because the British Government did not prevent the escape from a British port of the cruiser *Alabama*, built for the Confederacy, which subsequently preyed upon United States shipping. But Roosevelt brushed off objections based on international law with the off-the-cuff declaration:

"Such aid is not an act of war, even if a dictator should unilaterally proclaim it so to be."

The bill envisaged enormous and undefined expenditures and conferred vast and unprecedented discretionary powers upon the President. Its terms were to be effective "notwithstanding the provisions of any other law." But Roosevelt gave specific assurances that neither the Johnson Act, barring loans to countries in default on earlier obligations to the United States, nor the Neutrality Act, forbidding loans to belligerents, would be repealed.

Here was surely legal confusion heavily compounded. It was obvious that if the lend-lease bill should become law, the United States would have departed much farther from neutrality than Wilson had gone before America formally entered the First World War. Yet legislation enacted on the basis of America's experience in 1917, designed to keep the country out of war by foregoing neutral rights which Wilson had upheld, was left on the statute books. It was all very confusing; and confusion of public opinion was what Roosevelt needed gradually to steer

America into undeclared hostilities while professing devotion to peace. . . .

In retrospect the adoption of the Lend-Lease Act seems to be the most decisive of the series of moves which put America into an undeclared war in the Atlantic months before Japan struck at Pearl Harbor. This measure marked the end of any pretense of neutrality. It underwrote the unconditional victory of Britain with America's industrial power and natural resources. It opened up the immediate prospect of an appeal for naval action to insure that the munitions and supplies procured under lend-lease would reach England in spite of the submarine blockade. While Congress and the American people were being officially assured that lend-lease was not a move toward war, Roosevelt's personal envoy, Harry Hopkins, was giving Churchill the following categorical pledge of all-out American aid in January 1941: "The President is determined that we shall win the war together. Make no mistake about that."[5]

Yet this fateful measure was not frankly presented and advocated as equivalent to a state of limited belligerence. If one studies the record of the debates in House and Senate, one finds supporters of the bill employing this kind of reasoning:

"The present bill is a peace measure for our people."— Representative McCormack, of Massachusetts.

"In my judgment there is nothing in this bill which will hasten or accentuate our involvement in the war."— Representative Luther Johnson, of Texas.

"We believe that this measure offers the surest method by which we can avoid participation actively in this war and at the same time help those nations which are heroically grappling with a universal enemy and preserve the doctrines of our fathers and the aspirations of our own hearts."— Senator Alben Barkley, of Kentucky.

Leading Cabinet members and high military authorities testified on behalf of the bill and indulged in some very bad guessing. Frank Knox, Secretary of the Navy, predicted on January 17 a crisis within sixty days. On January 31 he forecast a great air blitz on Britain and the use of poison gas within sixty or ninety days. Stimson saw great danger of an airborne invasion and General Marshall predicted an attack on Great Britain in the spring. It is interesting to note that Churchill's authoritative memoirs do not bear out the alarmist arguments which were employed to push through the lend-lease bill. Describing the situation at the beginning of 1941, he points out in detail how British strength to resist a German invasion had immensely increased and states the following conclusion: "So long as there was no relaxation in vigilance or serious reduction in our own defense the War Cabinet and the Chiefs of Staff felt no anxiety."[6] Recurring to the situation in the spring of 1941, he observes: "I did not regard invasion as a serious danger in April, 1941, since proper preparations had been made against it."[7] . . .

A powerful voice from across the Atlantic joined the chorus of those who insisted that the lend-lease bill would keep America out of war. Winston Churchill, whose private letters to Roosevelt had long been filled with pleas for American warlike action, broadcast this reassurance to the American people on February 9, 1941:

We do not need the gallant armies which are forming throughout the American Union. We do not need them this year, nor next year, nor any year I can foresee. But we need

5 Winston Churchill, *The Grand Alliance* (Boston, Houghton, 1950), p. 23.

6 *Ibid.*, pp. 4–5.
7 *Ibid.*, p. 238.

urgently an immense and continuing supply of war materials. . . . We shall not fail or falter, we shall not weaken or tire. . . . *Give us the tools and we will do the job.* [Italics supplied.]

Viewing this broadcast in retrospect, Churchill frankly observes: "This could only be an interim pronouncement. Far more was needed. But we did our best."[8]

On any sober, realistic appraisal of British and Axis strength this was assurance which could not be fulfilled. But it was what many Americans wished to hear. Lend-lease was carried because the minority of all-out interventionists were reinforced by a larger number who hoped, and were given every assurance to this effect by Administration spokesmen, that unlimited subsidies of munitions and supplies would buy America out of active participation in the war.

There were voices of opposition. Senator Taft saw as "the important thing about this bill" that "its provisions in effect give the President power to carry on an undeclared war all over the world, in which America would do everything except actually put soldiers in the front-line trenches where the fighting is." The Senator could not see (and events would soon bear him out) how we could long conduct such a war without being in "the shooting as well as the service-of-supply end." Senator C. Wayland Brooks, of Illinois, called it a "war bill with war powers, with the deliberate intention of becoming involved in other peoples' wars." Colonel Lindbergh described lend-lease as "a major step to getting us into war." The veteran Socialist leader, Norman Thomas, foresaw as consequences of the lend-lease legislation "total war on two oceans and five continents; a war likely to result in stalemate, perhaps in

such a break-up of western civilization that Stalin, with his vast armies and loyal communist followers, will be the victor."

The bill became law on March 11, 1941. The vote was 265 to 165 in the House, 60 to 31 in the Senate. These were substantial, but not overwhelming majorities. Had the measure been frankly presented as a measure of limited war, which it was, it is most improbable that it could have been passed.

While Congress was discussing lend-lease, important American and British staff talks were taking place in Washington in an atmosphere of extreme secrecy.

At the very time when anxious Congressmen were being assured that the lend-lease bill was designed to avoid war, these military and naval experts were adopting a report which took American participation in the war for granted. The principal conclusions of this report were phrased as follows:

The staff conference assumes that *when* the United States becomes involved in war with Germany it will at the same time engage in war with Italy. In these circumstances the possibility of a state of war arising between Japan and an association of the United States, the British Commonwealth and its allies, including the Netherlands East Indies, must be taken into account.

Since Germany is the predominant member of the Axis powers, the Atlantic and European area is considered the decisive theatre. The principal United States effort will be exerted in that theatre, and operations in other theatres will be conducted in such a manner as to facilitate that effort.[9] [Italics supplied.]

The use of the word *when*, not *if*, was certainly suggestive of the Administration's attitude.

---

[8] *Ibid.*, p. 128.

[9] See JCC (Joint Congressional Committee on the Investigation of the Pearl Harbor Attack) Part 15, Ex. 49, 50, 51.

Typical of the furtive methods by which Roosevelt edged the country into a state of undeclared war was the noteworthy care taken to conceal these American-British talks (not only their content, but the fact that they were taking place) from the knowledge of Congress. This is made clear by Robert E. Sherwood when he writes:

Although the common-law alliance involved the United States in no undercover commitments, and no violation of the Constitution, the very existence of any American-British joint plans, however tentative, had to be kept utterly secret. It is an ironic fact that in all probability no great damage would have been done had the details of these plans fallen into the hands of the Germans and the Japanese; whereas, had they fallen into the hands of Congress and the press, American preparation for war might have been well nigh wrecked and ruined.[10]

There could scarcely be a more candid admission, from a source favorable to Roosevelt, that America was stealthily maneuvered into war behind the backs and without the knowledge of the elected representatives of the American people. A study of the Congressional debates and private talks with some members of that body confirm this view. Even members of the Senate and House Foreign Relations Committees were kept very much in the dark as to what the President was doing or intending to do. As Nathaniel Peffer subsequently wrote in an issue of *Harper's Magazine*:

When, for example, the United States traded to Great Britain destroyers for bases, it was for all practical purposes entering the war. Congress had no voice in that. It was notified later by the President, but then the fact was accomplished. Similarly, when the President ordered the freezing of Japanese assets in this country in July, 1941, he was decreeing a state of war with Japan. And with respect to that act the Senate Committee on Foreign Relations had no more to say than a similar number of North Dakota wheat farmers.[11]

Like the Roman god Janus, Roosevelt in the prewar period had two faces. For the American people, for the public record, there was the face of bland assurance that his first concern was to keep the country out of war. But in more intimate surroundings the Chief Executive often assumed that America was already involved in war. . . .

The next milestone on the road to war in the Atlantic was the decision to employ American naval forces to insure the deliveries of munitions and supplies to Britain. There had been much discussion of naval convoys during the debate on the Lend-Lease Act. Roosevelt stated on January 21 that he had no intention of using his powers under this bill to convoy merchant ships. "Convoys," he said, "mean shooting and shooting means war."

The Lend-Lease Act as finally passed contained several amendments clearly designed to prevent the President from using it as an authorization for carrying on undeclared war. According to these amendments, nothing in the Act was to authorize convoying by United States naval vessels, the entry of any American vessel into a combat area or the change of existing law relating to the use of the land and naval forces of the United States, "except insofar as such use relates to the manufacture, procurement and repair of defense articles, the communication of information and other noncombatant purposes enumerated in this act."

[10] *Roosevelt and Hopkins*, pp. 273–74.

[11] Nathaniel Peffer, "The Split in Our Foreign Policy," *Harper's Magazine*, 187 (August, 1943), p. 198.

As soon as the Lend-Lease Act became law Roosevelt characteristically set out to find a means of convoying supplies which could be plausibly called by some other name. "Patrol" seemed to fill the needs of the situation.

The bellicose Secretaries of War and the Navy, Stimson and Knox, had agreed toward the end of March "that the crisis is coming very soon and that convoying is the only solution and that it must come practically at once.[12] However, the plan which Roosevelt finally approved on April 24 was less bold than the open dispatch of convoys, although it achieved much the same purpose. Under this scheme the American Navy was assigned the responsibility of patrolling the Atlantic west of a median point represented by 25° longitude. Within this area United States warships and naval planes would search out German raiders and submarines and broadcast their position to the British Navy. Roosevelt and Hopkins drafted a cable to Churchill, outlining this scheme and suggesting that the British keep their convoys west of the new line up to the northwestern approaches.[13]

With typical indirection Roosevelt even in private Cabinet meetings tried to represent this as merely a defensive move, designed to protect the Western Hemisphere against attack. The more candid Stimson recorded in his diary for April 24:

He [Roosevelt] kept reverting to the fact that the forces in the Atlantic were merely going to be a patrol to watch for any aggression and report that to America. I answered there, with a smile on my face, saying: "But you are not going to report the presence of the German Fleet to the Americas. You are going to report it to the British Fleet." I wanted him to be honest with himself. To me it seems

[12] Henry L. Stimson and McGeorge Bundy, *On Active Service,* p. 367.
[13] Sherwood, *op. cit.,* pp. 291–92.

a clearly hostile act to the Germans, and I am prepared to take the responsibility of it. He seems to be trying to hide it into the character of a purely reconnaisance action, which it clearly is not.[14]

Even before the patrol system had been adopted, the American Navy had been stepping far beyond the bounds of hemisphere defense. The Congressional Pearl Harbor investigation turned up two interesting letters from Admiral Harold Stark, Chief of Naval Operations, to Admiral Husband E. Kimmel, commander in chief of the Pacific fleet. In the first of these, dated April 4, 1941, Stark wrote: "The question as to our entry into the war seems to be *when,* and not *whether.*" The second is more specific about military preparations on the other side of the Atlantic:

I am enclosing a memo on convoy which I drew up primarily to give the President a picture of what is now being done, what we would propose to do if we convoyed, and of our ability to do it. . . .

Our officers who have been studying the positions for bases in the British Isles have returned, and we have decided on immediate construction of 1 destroyer base and 1 seaplane base in Northern Ireland. We are also studying Scotland-Iceland bases for further support of the protective force for shipping in the northward approaches to Britain.

All this did not harmonize with the President's pre-election promises that "this country is not going to war." But with no election in prospect there was no brake on the gradual slide toward open belligerence.

Roosevelt in a press conference on May 16 referred to a subject which evidently appealed to his imagination, since he

[14] Stimson and Bundy, *op. cit.,* pp. 368–69.

raised it on several other occasions. This was the presidential right to wage undeclared war, as illustrated by such precedents as the clash with France during the Administration of John Adams and with the Barbary pirates when Jefferson was President. Roosevelt declared that the Germans were really pirates. On the same day Knox announced: "It is impossible to exaggerate the mortal danger of our country at this moment."

Stimson had already sounded a call to war in a radio address of May 6, which ended as follows:

Today a small group of evil leaders have taught the young men of Germany that the freedom of other men and nations must be destroyed. Today those young men are ready to die for that perverted conviction. Unless we on our side are ready to sacrifice and, if need be, die for the conviction that the freedom of America must be saved, it will not be saved. Only by a readiness for the same sacrifice can that freedom be preserved.

Roosevelt himself on May 27, 1941, delivered a speech which seemed designed to scare the American people into approving warlike measures. "The war," the President said, "is approaching the brink of the Western Hemisphere itself. It is coming very close to home." He spoke of "the Nazi book of world conquest" and declared the Nazis planned to treat the Latin American countries as they were now treating the Balkans. Then, according to the President, the United States and Canada would be strangled. American labor would have to compete with slave labor and the American farmer would get for his products exactly what Hitler wanted to give. Roosevelt outlined a very elastic and expansive conception of defense requirements.

"The attack on the United States can begin with the domination of any base which menaces our security — north or south."

Therefore:

Old-fashioned common sense calls for the use of a strategy that will prevent such an enemy from gaining a foothold in the first place.

We have, accordingly, extended our patrol in North and South Atlantic waters. We are steadily adding more and more ships and planes to that patrol. It is well known that the strength of the Atlantic Fleet has been greatly increased during the last year, and that it is constantly being built up. . . .[15] We are thus being forewarned. We shall be on our guard against efforts to establish Nazi bases closer to our hemisphere.

The speech ended in a bellicose climax:

We in the Americas will decide for ourselves whether, and when, and where, our American interests are attacked or our security is threatened.

We are placing our armed forces in strategic military position.

We will not hesitate to use our armed forces to repel attack.

There was also a declaration of a state of "unlimited national emergency." However, there was a sense of anticlimax when Roosevelt in his press conference on the following day denied any intention to institute convoys or to press for the repeal of the Neutrality Act.

In the retrospect of years, how well founded was the sense of national mortal peril which the President, the more bellicose members of his Cabinet, and a host of individuals and organizations tried to cultivate in the American people? In the light of the ascertainable facts, which are now pretty well known, one cannot

---

[15] This fact was doubtless "well known" to the Japanese Intelligence Service and was one consideration which prompted the attack on Pearl Harbor.

but feel that the picture was grossly exaggerated.

What was the over-all military picture in May 1941? There was no longer serious danger of a Nazi invasion of England.[16] The American and British surface fleets were enormously stronger than the combined Axis naval strength. There was, therefore, not the slightest prospect that German armies could cross the Atlantic in force.

At that time there were constant rumors of German infiltration into French North Africa. A favorite scare story was that Hitler's legions would move into Dakar (itself a long jump from North Africa) and then move across the Atlantic into Brazil. Commentators who spread these stories never took the trouble to explain how it would be possible to transport substantial forces across the ocean in the face of superior American and British naval power.

And we know now that there was never any factual basis for these rumors. The reports of two American representatives on the spot, Robert D. Murphy, in North Africa, and Consul Thomas C. Wasson, in Dakar, are in agreement on this point; Murphy's reports show that there were about two hundred Germans, mostly connected with the armistice commission, in North Africa. Wasson informed the State Department that the only Germans in Dakar were a few Jewish refugees.[17]

The fall of Germany and the capture of the Nazi archives revealed no evidence of any plan for the invasion of North or South America. It is reasonable to assume that a victorious Nazi Germany would have been an uncomfortable neighbor, just as a victorious Soviet Russia is today. But there is no proof that Hitler envis-

aged the American continent as part of his empire.

And there is a strong element of overheated fantasy in the vision of American labor ground down by the competition of slave labor, of the American farmer condemned to take what Hitler would give. The Nazis could scarcely have made slave labor more prevalent than it is in Stalin's huge postwar empire. American labor standards have not been depressed as a result. And the level of American farm prices depends far more on the state of supply and on the willingness of American taxpayers to pay subsidies than it does on the character of foreign political regimes.

Unquestionably the war was not going well for Britain in the spring of 1941. The Germans had overrun the Balkans and had seized Crete by an air-borne operation. The reconquest of Europe from Hitler and the crushing of the Nazi regime in its own territory, the obvious war aim of Churchill and Roosevelt, gave every prospect of being a difficult, long, and costly enterprise.

But the suggestion that the Western Hemisphere was in imminent peril can fairly be dismissed as a fraudulent exaggeration. The fraud and the exaggeration are all the greater if one considers that both the American and the British governments were in possession of reliable information to the effect that Hitler's main military strength would soon be hurled against Russia. The most fevered alarmist imagination could scarcely envisage Hitler's simultaneously invading Russia and mounting an offensive against the American continent.

Not all Americans were convinced by the dire forebodings of Roosevelt's "unlimited national emergency" speech. Senator Taft commented drily in a nationwide broadcast:

---

[16] This point is recognized by Churchill several times in *The Grand Alliance*.

[17] William L. Langer, *Our Vichy Gamble*, p. 87.

The whole argument of the war party that Hitler can conquer the United States or dominate the seas that surround us has just about faded into the discard. But the President now lays more stress on the danger to our trade. He threatens the American workman that his wages and hours would be fixed by Hitler. . . . What is Japan to do with its silk except sell it to us? We take over half Brazil's coffee. Even if the Nazis dominated the Netherlands East Indies there would be nothing to do with the rubber except sell it to us. It is utterly ridiculous to suppose that our trade with South America or Asia or even Europe will be wiped out.

Hitler's attack on Russia gave the war an entirely new character. Now there was a gigantic duel between two dictators for the mastery of a continent from which every other strong military power had been eliminated. From the standpoint of defeating Hitler Russia was a valuable military asset. But this military advantage was offset by grave political risks. There was nothing in the Soviet political record to suggest the likelihood of respect for the Four Freedoms, or of the ideals later formulated in the Atlantic Charter.

On the contrary, there was every prospect that a victorious Soviet Union would be as ruthless in victory, as eager to expand as a victorious Germany. There was neither moral nor political advantage in substituting Stalin for Hitler.

Curiously enough, it was a man of no experience in foreign affairs who sensed the necessity for a careful handling of the Soviet Union as an associate. Senator Harry S. Truman was quoted in the *New York Times* of June 23, 1941, as saying:

If we see Germany is winning we ought to help Russia and if we see Russia is winning we ought to help Germany, and in that way let them kill as many as possible, although I wouldn't want to see Hitler victorious under

any circumstances. Neither of them think [*sic*] anything of their pledged word.

But the official decision, in Washington as in London, was to go all-out in aid to Stalin. There was apparently no thought of requiring, as the price of this aid, that Stalin renounce the spoils of his pact with Hitler and give specific binding guarantees against Soviet annexation of foreign territory. . . .

Roosevelt approved the trip and Hopkins flew to Moscow with Churchill's blessing late in July. On meeting Stalin he told the Soviet dictator that Roosevelt considered Hitler the enemy of mankind and therefore wished to aid the Soviet Union in its fight against Germany. Hopkins impressed upon Stalin America's determination to extend all possible aid to the Soviet Union.

Stalin took a moral tone in his reply. The Germans, he said, were a people who would sign a treaty today and break it tomorrow. Nations must fulfill their treaty obligations or international society could not exist.[18]

Here was a moment when Hopkins might well have suggested that the Soviet Government, like the Nazi Government, had been known to break treaties and that a solemn public pledge to restore the independence and territorial integrity of Poland, Finland, and the Baltic states would be a reasonable *quid pro quo* for American aid. But neither then nor at any other time did Hopkins show any awareness of the bargaining possibilities of lend-lease aid. His whole attitude was that of one who had come to seek a favor, not to confer one. It was not a happy psychological approach to a tough-minded dictator. . . .

From his conferences with Stalin, Hopkins was flown back to London.

[18] Sherwood, *op. cit.*, p. 328.

Thence he proceeded to take part in the first wartime meeting between Roosevelt and Churchill. This meeting, prepared in the greatest secrecy, took place on warships in the harbor of Argentia, in Newfoundland, one of the bases which the United States had acquired in exchange for its destroyers. . . .

Since the principles of the Atlantic Charter were repeatedly reaffirmed not only by America and Great Britain, but by the Soviet Union and other members of the United Nations coalition, it may be regarded as a morally binding statement of the ideals which should have governed the making of the peace. The first three clauses restate a familiar Wilsonian idea: the right of all peoples to choose their national allegiance and form of government.

Clause 4 is a promise of equality in commercial opportunity between nations. Other objectives of the Charter are the promotion of improved social and economic conditions, the insuring of a stable peace, the disarming of "aggressor" nations.

Churchill was later to contend that the provisions of the Charter did not apply to Germany. But this is in contradiction to the plain wording of the document. Clause 4 refers to "all states, great or small, *victor or vanquished* [italics supplied]," and Clause 6 mentions "all the men in all the lands."

There were two disagreements regarding the phrasing of the Charter. The qualifying phrase, "with due respect for their existing obligations," was inserted by Churchill at the insistence of Lord Beaverbrook, a staunch champion of Empire economic preferences. Clause 6 in its original form included the words "by effective international organization." These were struck out by Roosevelt because of fear of opposition which might be aroused in the United States.

Another important subject at the con-

ference was American and British diplomatic action against Japan. Churchill pressed for a joint threat of war. From his standpoint it would be just as well if America got into the war in the Pacific as in the Atlantic. So the draft of the declaration which Roosevelt was supposed to address to the Japanese Government, as submitted by Cadogan, contained the ultimate specific threat. It read:

1. Any further encroachment by Japan in the Southwestern Pacific would produce a situation in which the United States Government would be compelled to take countermeasures even though these might lead to war between the United States and Japan.

2. If any third power becomes the object of aggression by Japan in consequence of such counter-measures or of their support of them, the President would have the intention to seek authority from Congress to give aid to such power.

However, on reflection Roosevelt considerably softened this statement. When he received Japanese Ambassador Nomura on August 17 the warning had been watered down to vaguer and more oblique terms:

This Government now finds it necessary to say to the Government of Japan that if the Japanese Government takes any further steps in pursuance of a policy or program of military domination by force or threat of force of neighboring countries the Government of the United States will be compelled to take immediately any and all steps which it may deem necessary toward safeguarding the legitimate rights and interests of the United States and American nationals and toward insuring the safety and security of the United States.

There was also an agreement during the Roosevelt-Churchill meeting that the United States should occupy the Azores Islands, while Great Britain proposed to take over the Canary and Cape Verde Islands.[19] The Cape Verde Islands were to be transferred to American occupation later. This plan never went into effect because the rumored German move into the Iberian peninsula which inspired the design to seize the islands in the East Atlantic never took place.

In view of the agreements about a joint warning to Japan and about military action on the foreign soil of the East Atlantic islands, Roosevelt was not candid when he declared after the conference that there were no new commitments and that the country was no closer to war. To be sure, something had occurred on the last day of the conference which was calculated to impose a brake on a too-headlong interventionist course. The renewal of the Selective Service Act, enacted in 1940 for one year, squeezed through the House of Representatives by only one vote. . . .

Roosevelt's next move toward war in the Atlantic was the proclamation, without consulting Congress or obtaining congressional sanction, of a "shoot at sight" campaign against Axis submarines. The pretext was an exchange of shots between the *Greer,* an American destroyer bound for Iceland, and a German submarine on September 5. Roosevelt misrepresented this incident as a wanton, unprovoked attack on the American vessel. . . .

Bismarck's editing of the Ems telegram was a masterpiece of straightforwardness compared with Roosevelt's picture of the *Greer* as the peaceful mail-carrier, wantonly set on by a hostile submarine. The Senate Naval Affairs Committee looked into the matter and obtained the following account of the incident from Admiral Stark:

At 8:40 A.M. a British airplane notified the *Greer* that a submarine was sub-

merged ten miles ahead on the course the destroyer was following. The *Greer* put on speed and zigzagged its way to the reported location. As soon as its sound detection apparatus picked up the propeller beat of the submarine the destroyer commenced to track the submarine, broadcasting its location for the benefit of any British airplanes and destroyers which might be in the vicinity.

"This," said Admiral Stark, "was in accordance with her orders, that is to give out information, but not to attack."

At 10:32 the airplane dropped four depth charges which missed their mark and twenty minutes later withdrew from the hunt. The *Greer* continued to trail the submarine. At 12:40 the German vessel changed its course, closed in on the *Greer,* and fired a torpedo, which missed. The *Greer* counterattacked, apparently without success.

The announcement of the Presidential shooting war in the Atlantic was followed by more serious clashes. The destroyer *Kearny* was hit by a torpedo with the loss of eleven lives on October 17 and on October 30 the *Reuben James,* another destroyer, was sunk with a casualty list of 155 members of her crew.

Roosevelt struck a new high bellicose note in his Navy Day speech of October 27:

The shooting has started. And history has recorded who fired the first shot. In the long run, however, all that will matter is who fired the last shot. . . .

I say that we do not propose to take this lying down.

Today, in the face of this newest and greatest challenge of them all, we Americans have cleared our decks and taken our battle stations. We stand ready in the defense of our nation and the faith of our fathers to do what God has given us the power to see as our full duty.

But the majority of the American

[19] The Azores and Cape Verde groups belong to Portugal, the Canary Islands to Spain.

people remained markedly indifferent to these warlike appeals. The contrast between the President's categorical pledges not to get into war in 1940 (when the danger to Britain was certainly far greater than it was after Hitler attacked Russia) and his present obvious efforts to get into hostilities at any price was too strong.

Some public-opinion polls taken during this period are not very revealing. Much depended on who was conducting them, on how questions were phrased, on which groups in the community were reached. But Congress was a pretty reliable barometer of the mood of the nation. The one-vote majority by which selective service was renewed was one signal of the aversion to the idea of a second crusade. Another unmistakable signal was given only three weeks before Pearl Harbor.

The President had asked for authority to arm American merchant ships and to send these ships into war zones. This amounted to a repeal of the Neutrality Act, which Roosevelt had done everything in his power to circumvent. This proposal was still far short of a declaration of war. But it proved extremely difficult to get legislation providing for these changes through Congress. The bill passed the Senate, 50–37, on November 7 and narrowly escaped defeat in the House, where the vote was 212–194, a week later. A change of ten votes would have given the Administration a severe setback. Very strong pressure from the White House was put on the representatives, including promises of judgeships and other federal appointments where these would do the most good.

Interventionists at this time freely admitted and deplored the reluctance of the American people to plunge into the slaughter. The Committee to Defend America by Aiding the Allies took a full-page advertisement to lament the "dreadfully narrow margin" by which the bill authorizing the arming of merchant ships had passed. Walter Lippmann wrote in September 1941 of "the low state of our war morale." Stanley High, another publicist who favored intervention, commented regretfully on Lippmann's observation in a letter published in the *New York Herald Tribune:*

"No, the whole truth about our war morale is not that it is now in a slump. Measured by what we are up against, it was never in anything else."

An investigation of the alleged attempt of the moving-picture industry to promote a war psychosis was started in the Senate in September. John T. Flynn, one of the active leaders of the America First Committee, accused film producers of "using propaganda to raise the war hysteria in this country, to inflame the people of the United States to a state of mind where they will be willing to go to war with Germany." He cited *Underground* as one of some fifty films designed to arouse feelings of hatred and vengeance.

The radio and the press, like the films, were overwhelmingly on the interventionist side by the autumn of 1941. Flynn asserted that in three days he had counted 127 interventionist broadcasts, compared with six on the other side.

And yet, with all the sparks that were being generated, the people failed to catch fire. Hundreds of chapters of the America First Committee pledged themselves to work for the defeat of congressmen who had voted to repeal the Neutrality Act. Francis P. Miller, an extreme interventionist, was defeated by a Republican in an off-year election in Fairfax County, Virginia, in November 1941. This was a district in which a Democratic victory was normally taken for granted.

The autumn of 1941 was a difficult period for Roosevelt. He was under pressure from those members of his Cabinet, Stimson and Knox and Morgenthau, who favored stronger action. He was exposed to a barrage of transatlantic pleas from Churchill. He had stretched his Presidential powers to the limit. He had provoked shooting incidents in the Atlantic and misrepresented these incidents when they occurred. But he had not aroused much will to war in the country.

General Wood, chairman of the America First Committee, challenged Roosevelt to put the issue of a declaration of war to the test of a vote in Congress. This was a challenge which the President could not accept, in view of the close vote on the less provocative question of repealing the Neutrality Act. Robert E. Sherwood tells how gloomy the situation seemed at this time to those who wished to get America into the war:

The truth was that, as the world situation became more desperately critical, and as the limitless peril came closer and closer to the United States, isolationist sentiment became ever more strident in expression and aggressive in action, and Roosevelt was relatively powerless to combat it. He had said everything "short of war" that could be said. He had no more tricks left. The hat from which he had pulled so many rabbits was empty.[20]

But just when the situation in the Atlantic seemed very unpromising, from the standpoint of speedy full involvement in war, rescue for the Administration came from the Pacific. The Japanese attack on Pearl Harbor, followed by Hitler's declaration of war, extricated Roosevelt from one of the most difficult dilemmas in which a statesman can find himself — the dilemma of having led his people halfway into war.

[20] Sherwood, *op. cit.,* pp. 382–83.

The eleven principal steps by which Roosevelt took America into undeclared war in the Atlantic may be briefly summarized as follows:

(1) The repeal of the arms embargo in November 1939.

(2) The trade of destroyers for bases in September 1940.

(3) Enactment of the Lend-Lease Act in March 1941.

(4) The secret American-British staff talks, January-March 1941.

(5) The institution of "patrols" in the North Atlantic on April 24.

(6) The sending of American laborers to build a naval base in Northern Ireland.

(7) The blocking of German credits in the United States and the closing of consulates in the early summer of 1941.

(8) The occupation of Iceland by American troops on July 7.

(9) The Atlantic Conference, August 9–12.

(10) The shoot-at-sight orders given to American warships and announced on September 11.

(11) Authorization for the arming of merchant ships and the sending of merchant ships into war zones in November 1941.

The first three of these steps were accompanied by loud protestations that they were designed to keep America at peace, not to get it into war. Several of the other measures were taken without consulting Congress in an atmosphere of exaggerated alarmism, secrecy, contrived confusion and official misrepresentation of facts. The entire record may be usefully set against Roosevelt's repeated categorical assurances that his principal aim was to keep America out of war. Seldom if ever in American history was there such a gulf between appearances and realities, between Presidential words and Presidential deeds.

Charles Callan Tansill: BACK DOOR TO WAR

THE FAR EAST IN FERMENT

A Triple Offensive Is Launched against Japan

WHILE the Roosevelt Administration was putting its diplomatic house in order with reference to Nazi Germany, the situation in the Far East constantly threatened to get out of hand. The heritage of the Stimson policy was an unfortunate one. But the policy of pressure upon Japan antedated Stimson some two decades. Dollar diplomacy under Taft challenged Japan's position in Manchuria, and under Woodrow Wilson a three-pronged offensive was launched against Nippon. The first phase of this offensive began when Japan presented to China in January 1915 the famous Twenty-One Demands. In connection with these demands the American Minister at Peking, Paul Reinsch, sent to the Department of State a series of dispatches so critical in tone that they helped to create in American minds a fixation of Japanese wickedness that made eventual war a probability.[1] This probability was increased when Secretary Bryan (May 11, 1915) sent to Tokyo a nonrecognition note that was later exhumed from the old files of State Department correspondence by Secretary Stimson and fashioned into a hand grenade that shattered all hope of peaceful relations between Japan and the United States.

In 1917, when America intervened in World War I, the single-track mind of President Wilson was directed towards Europe. Japan suddenly became our little brown brother in a crusade against the sinister designs of the Central Powers. She was to be courted instead of criticized and her help to the Allies could be paid in terms of a new understanding of Japan's special position in North China. Britain, France, and Russia had already in the early months of 1917 signed secret treaties with Japan which pledged their support of her claims to the retention of the German rights in Shantung and the German islands north of the equator.[2] When America entered the war Balfour paid a visit to Washington and informed both President Wilson and Secretary Lansing of the terms of the secret treaties.[3] As Professor Griswold sagely remarked: "It is hard to escape the conclusion that those [treaties] relating to Shantung were among Balfour's revelations."[4] As a matter of fact, Lansing, in his *Diary*, frankly admits that he knew the terms

[1] Paul W. Reinsch, *An American Diplomat in China* (New York, 1922), chap. 12; Thomas E. La Fargue, *China and the World War* (Stanford, 1937), chap. 3.

[2] F. Seymour Cocks, *The Secret Treaties and Understandings* (London, 1918), pp. 84–88; J. V. A. MacMurray, *Treaties and Agreements with and Concerning China* (New York, 1921), II, 1168–69.

[3] Blanche E. Dugdale, *Arthur James Balfour* (New York, 1936), II, 145–46. See also, Balfour to President Wilson, January 31, 1918, File 2, Box 135. Wilson Papers, Library of Congress; and Secretary Lansing to President Wilson, November 18, 1918, File 2, Box 156. *Ibid.*

[4] A. Whitney Griswold, *The Far Eastern Policy of the United States* (New York, 1938), p. 219.

From *Back Door to War: The Roosevelt Foreign Policy, 1933–1941* by Charles Callan Tansill (Chicago: Henry Regnery Company), excerpted material from pages 51–429. Reprinted by permission.

of the secret treaty between Britain and Japan: "The problem of the final disposition of Germany's colonial possessions should be considered as unsettled. . . . In the case of the Pacific islands I learned last summer that Japan and Great Britain have a secret agreement by which Japan shall retain after the war the German territories north of the equator."[5]

On November 2, 1917, Lansing and Viscount Ishii signed the well-known Lansing-Ishii Agreement which specifically stated that "territorial propinquity creates special relations between countries, and consequently, the Government of the United States recognizes that Japan has special interests in China, particularly in the part to which her possessions are contiguous." With reference to this agreement, Professor Griswold makes the following comment:

Established diplomatic usage has endowed the phrase "special interests" with political as well as economic connotations. . . . The situation in world politics at the time the agreement was being negotiated was such as to suggest that Lansing realized the political character of his concession and concealed it. . . . The fact is, Lansing knew of the existence of the secret treaties, with which his phrase was pale in comparison and which rendered fantastic the expectations implicit in the rest of the agreement. . . . Given Lansing's knowledge of the Allied commitments to Japan, even the phrase "special interests" implied at least tentative recognition of them.[6]

When one keeps these facts in mind, it is evident that the policy of the President at Paris was a most dubious one. During the sessions of the Peace Conference he led a determined assault upon the Japanese position in Shantung in the face of

his acquiescence in the secret treaty that bound Britain to support the Japanese claims to economic domination of that province. The Lansing-Ishii Agreement had formally recorded this acquiescence. Wilson's action, therefore, and his subsequent denial of any knowledge of the secret treaties must have convinced Japanese statesmen that he was implementing the maxims of Machiavelli.

Another aspect of the President's offensive against Japan had to do with Allied intervention in Siberia in 1918. During the spring of that year the Allied governments kept urging the United States to consent to a proposal to have Japan send an expeditionary force into Siberia as "a mandatory of the Powers." . . .

As a result of numerous conferences dealing with the Far East it was finally decided to send General William S. Graves with a small army (9,014 officers and men) to Siberia to co-operate with an Allied expeditionary force. The duties assigned to this force were to assist the Czechs, help steady genuine Russian efforts at self-government and self-defense, and to guard Allied military stores. The force under Graves stayed in Siberia from August 1918 until April 1920. Its sole achievement was to save the maritime provinces of Siberia from the ruthless rule of Red Russia.[7]

The third thrust of the Wilson offensive against Japan took the form of financial pressure. During the Taft Administration certain American banks were high-pressured into participating in the Chinese Hukuang Railways loan. This action meant American membership in a four-power banking consortium. The status of

[5] Lansing *Diary*, January 10, 1918. Lansing Papers, Library of Congress.

[6] Griswold, *op. cit.*, pp. 218–19.

[7] General William S. Graves, *America's Siberian Adventure* (New York, 1931); Pauline Tompkins, *American-Russian Relations in the Far East* (New York, 1949), pp. 47–141; John A. White, *The Siberian Intervention* (Princeton, 1950), pp. 270–74.

this participation was carefully defined in the agreements of November 10, 1910, and May 20, 1911.[8] In 1912 (June 18–20) Japan and Russia joined this banking group making it a six-power consortium. . . .

The outbreak of the World War eliminated Germany and Russia from the consortium, and Britain and France were so heavily burdened by the costs of war that they were unable to extend any loans to China. Japan quickly moved into this financial vacuum and loaned to China more than 320,000,000 yen.[9] . . .

On June 22, Secretary Lansing invited the representatives of important banking groups to discuss with him the formation of a new consortium. They promptly accepted this invitation and on October 8 the Department of State formally outlined to the governments of Britain, France, and Japan a detailed proposal for a new consortium.[10] On March 17, 1919,[11] the British Government accepted the American proposal, but France and Japan delayed favorable action. The Japanese press was opposed to the new consortium on the ground that it would mean the loss by Japan of the "fruits she had amassed" in the past few years.[12] The Japanese Government entertained similar fears

and Mr. Odagiri, the Japanese financial representative at Paris, was instructed to inform Mr. Thomas W. Lamont, chief American financial representative, that "all rights and options held by Japan in the regions of Manchuria and Mongolia, where Japan has special interests, should be excluded from the arrangement."[13]

Lamont immediately informed Odagiri that any attempt to exclude Manchuria and Mongolia from the scope of the new consortium would be "inadmissible."[14] He also wrote to J. P. Morgan and Company and expressed the opinion that there was no hope that Japan would recede from her position unless "the United States and Great Britain will assume a very rigorous position in the matter."[15] From Peking the American Minister warned that the Japanese were playing their "usual game" of deceit. Probably "you are being assured that they are favorable to the consortium and will join it in due course. Meanwhile influence is exerted to stir up the Chinese against it."[16]

In order to exert pressure upon the Japanese Government the Department of State toyed with the idea of a three-power consortium, but Britain and France were opposed to such a move.[17] Undue pressure upon Japan might propel her into an alliance with Germany.[18]

[8] Frederick V. Field, *American Participation in the China Consortiums* (Chicago, 1931), pp. 14–66; John G. Reid, *The Manchu Abdication and the Powers, 1908–1912* (Berkeley, 1935), pp. 36–241, 258–99.

[9] *Foreign Relations, 1918*, pp. 167–68.

[10] Secretary Lansing to Ambassador Jusserand, October 8, 1918. 893.51/2042e, MS, Department of State.

[11] British Foreign Office to the American Embassy, London, March 17, 1919. *The Consortium: The Official Text of the Four-Power Agreement for a Loan to China and Relevant Documents* (Washington, 1921), No. 5, p. 15.

[12] Ambassador Morris to Secretary Lansing, Tokyo, May 28, 1919. 893.51/2241, MS, Department of State.

[13] J. W. Davis to Acting Secretary Polk, London, June 18, 1919. 893.51/2268, MS. Department of State.

[14] J. P. Morgan and Company to Dept. of State, June 25, 1919. 893.51/2282, MS, Department of State.

[15] T. W. Lamont to J. P. Morgan and Company. 893.51/2268, MS, Department of State.

[16] Reinsch to Secretary Lansing, Peking, June 26, 1919. 893.51/2284, MS, Department of State.

[17] Ambassador Wallace to Breckinridge Long, Paris, July 13, 1919. 893.51/2308, MS, Department of State.

[18] Ambassador Wallace to Secretary Lansing, Paris, September 16, 1919. 893.51/2425, MS, Department of State.

In an endeavor to explain their desire to exclude Manchuria and Mongolia from the scope of this proposed consortium, the Japanese Government pointed out that those regions were of vital interest from the viewpoint of national defense. Recent developments in Russia were a matter of "grave concern." The situation in Siberia might take a sudden turn that would threaten "the safety of Japan," and ultimately all eastern Asia might become the victim of the "sinister activities of extremist forces."[19]

Secretary Lansing could understand this Japanese fear of the onward tide of bolshevism. With reference to Japan's desire to station adequate forces in Siberia for the purpose of checking that tide he made the following comment in his diary:

My belief is that they [the Japanese] will send reinforcements to Siberia and attempt to strengthen Seminoff's force [of White Russians]. I cannot see how the Japanese Government can adopt any other policy in view of the very real peril to Japan if the Bolsheviks should gain a foothold in Manchuria and co-operate with the Korean revolutionists. Certainly in the circumstances we ought not to raise any objection to Japan sending a sufficient force to check the Bolshevik advance, for the spread of Bolshevism in the Far East would be a dreadful menace to civilization.[20]

During the very months while the consortium negotiations were going on, Lansing made another illuminating entry in his diary:

I have little patience with these people who are forever on the verge of hysterics about the deep and wicked schemes of Japan. They

imagine some of the most preposterous things and report them as facts. I would be inclined to think that some of these enemies of Japan were mentally unbalanced but for their sanity on all other subjects. Unfortunately, they are listened to by many Americans whose reason ought to warn them against believing such tales without better evidence.[21]

Ambassador Morris, in Tokyo, joined with Secretary Lansing in lending a sympathetic ear to Japanese representations concerning their need to build strong bastions of defense in North China. He believed that the "strong, fundamental, tenacious purpose" of the Japanese Government was to assure protection of their lines of communication with sources of raw materials and foodstuffs. America should give "consideration" to the Japanese viewpoint: "Unless we do so the likelihood of solving the existing problems is scant."[22]

Financiers talk more abruptly than diplomats. Mr. Lamont thought that it would be

poor policy to give the Japanese Government any further leeway in this matter. In my judgment they ought to be down on their knees in gratitude to the American, British and French groups for inviting the Japanese group to become a partner and for being so patient in the matter. My associates and I are agreed that the best thing is to bring them up with a round turn and if they do not like it, let them go their way.[23]

The Department of State swung round to the viewpoint of Mr. Lamont and the British Foreign Office did the same. In the face of this pressure the Japanese

---

[19] Japanese Embassy to the Department of State, March 2, 1920. 893.51/2695, MS, Department of State.

[20] Lansing, *op. cit.*, November 30, 1918.

[21] *Ibid.*, July 31, 1919.

[22] Ambassador Morris to Acting Secretary Polk, March 11, 1920. 893.51/2707, MS, Department of State.

[23] Ambassador Morris to Secretary Colby, Tokyo, April 8, 1920, with inclosures. 893.51/2765, MS, Department of State.

Government made some concessions and the new consortium agreement was finally signed on October 15, 1920.[24] The number of exceptions that Japan insisted upon were significant and this fact made the Chinese Government lukewarm in its attitude towards the consortium. In January 1921 the Chinese Foreign Office was notified of the new consortium agreement but no answer to this notification was ever sent from Peiping. In his *Preliminary Report on the New Consortium for China,* Mr. Lamont spoke in his usual blunt fashion:

If . . . the leading Powers, under whose approval the New Consortium has been organized, should make to the present Peking Government, to the Southern Government and to all factions in China including the Tuchuns, strong diplomatic representations stating that all this nonsense of an *opera bouffe* warfare must be dropped and the Government must get down to business, I am inclined to believe that the result would be surprising in its effectiveness.[25]

But the four powers represented in the new consortium were not inclined to accept the forthright advice of Mr. Lamont. They were content to remain on the sidelines while rival factions in China feverishly undermined the national structure. If Mr. Lamont's bold words had been implemented by some form of effective intervention there may have been some chance for Chinese salvation, but the consortium Powers merely waited for opportunities that never came. Shunned by the rapidly changing governments in China, the consortium accomplished nothing. Nationalist China rejected with hot contempt any thought of surrendering the slightest portion of her sovereignty to international bankers. Moreover, a powerful communist leaven was busily working in China, and the most powerful leader in turbulent Canton was Sun Yat-sen who had a strong leftist inclination. The Kremlin lost no time in exploiting this inclination. . . .

CONTINUED FRICTION WITH JAPAN POINTS TOWARDS INEVITABLE WAR

Congress Enacts an Exclusion Law Which Angers Japan

As American statesmen looked from the troubled scenes in China to the quiet landscapes in Japan, it was not with relief but with suspicion that they viewed the placid picture of Old Nippon. The orderly ways of empire grated upon the sensibilities of many Americans who pre-

ferred the uneasy atmosphere of democracy to the regulated rhythm of the Mikado's Government. Since 1913, Japan had been under almost constant attack by the Department of State. The Wilson Administration had led a sustained assault against Japan along several fronts, and the inauguration of a Republican Administration in 1921 had led to the

[24] In a letter to Nakaji Kajiwara, president of the Yokohama Specie Bank, May 11, 1920, Mr. Lamont listed the terms agreed upon: "(1) that the South Manchuria Railway and its present branches, together with mines which are subsidiary to the railway, do not come within the

scope of the Consortium; (2) that the projected Taonanfu-Jehol Railway and the projected railway connecting a point on the Taonanfu-Jehol Railway with a seaport are to be included within the terms of the Consortium."

[25] Pp. 14–15.

calling of the Washington Conference for the express purpose of checking Japanese plans for expansion. The climate of opinion in the United States was definitely hostile to Japan, and it was inevitable that clouds of misunderstanding between the two countries should gather along the diplomatic horizon. The first threat of a storm came in connection with the immigration question.

After the close of the World War there was an increasing fear in the United States that the war-impoverished countries of Europe would send a huge wave of immigration to American shores. On May 19, 1921, in order to prevent such a contingency, Congress enacted a law that limited the number of aliens of any particular nationality that would be granted admission to the United States in any one year to 3 per cent of the "number of foreign-born persons of such nationality resident in the United States" in the year 1910. Some months later a new act was framed which reduced the annual admission of any nationality to 2 per cent of the foreign-born population of that nationality resident in the United States in 1890.[26] A high dyke had been erected against the expected wave of immigration.

It was soon apparent that this new legislation would not be used merely to supplement the gentlemen's agreement with Japan which since 1907 had controlled the immigration of laborers from that country. In 1921 a movement began in the Far West to exclude by legislation any further immigration of Japanese laborers. This could be accomplished by employing a phrase suggested in 1922 by the Supreme Court when it ruled that Japanese were ineligible for citizenship by naturalization. Federal legislation

could be framed so that it would apply solely to Japanese immigrants.[27]

In December 1923, bills were introduced in Congress prohibiting the admission of aliens ineligible for citizenship. The Japanese Ambassador promptly voiced a strong protest. In the eyes of the Foreign Office it was necessary to know "whether Japan as a nation is or is not entitled to the proper respect and consideration of other nations."[28]

On February 8, Secretary Hughes sent a long letter to Representative Albert Johnson, chairman of the House Committee on Immigration, in which he criticized the proposed legislation as inconsistent with the treaty of 1911. It would also "largely undo the work of the Washington Conference on Limitation of Armament, which so greatly improved our relations with Japan." He was certain that it was not "worth while thus to affront a friendly nation with whom we have established the most cordial relations."[29]

While this letter of protest was resting quietly in a pigeonhole in Mr. Johnson's desk, Secretary Hughes and Ambassador Hanihara were exchanging notes on the immigration issue. Hanihara insisted that his country had no intention of "questioning the sovereign right of any country to regulate immigration to its own territories." He could not, however, understand the need for a measure that would "not only seriously offend the just pride of a friendly nation . . . but would also involve the question of the good faith and therefore of the honor of their govern-

[26] A. Whitney Griswold, *The Far Eastern Policy of the United States.* (New York, 1938), pp. 369–70.

[27] *Ibid.,* p. 369.

[28] The Japanese Embassy to the Department of State, January 15, 1924. 711.945/1063, MS, Department of State.

[29] Secretary Hughes to the chairman of the Committee on Immigration and Naturalization of the House of Representatives, February 8, 1924. 150.01/778, MS, Department of State.

ment." The enactment of the proposed legislation might lead to "grave consequences" which he hoped might be avoided by another type of restriction.[30]

When Secretary Hughes sent this correspondence to Congress, Senator Lodge declared that the phrase "grave consequences" was a "veiled threat" which should be answered by the immediate passage of the exclusion law. When this suggestion was acted upon by both houses of Congress, Hanihara wrote to Secretary Hughes and asserted that he was "unable to understand how the two words, read in their context, could be construed as meaning anything like a threat."[31] Hughes agreed with the ambassador's viewpoint and then wrote to Senator Lodge to express the opinion that an irreparable injury had been done, "not to Japan but to ourselves." It had been most unwise to arouse in the minds of large numbers of Japanese a feeling of bitter resentment against the United States: "I dislike to think what the reaping will be after the sowing of this seed."[32] . . .

Background of the Manchurian Incident

JAPAN IS WORRIED OVER THE SPREAD OF COMMUNISM IN CHINA. The outcome of the conflict between China and Soviet Russia in 1929 had important implications for Japan. First of all, it was clear that Russia had violated the provisions of the Sino-Russian agreement of 1924 which prohibited the spread of communistic propaganda in China. The vast amount of data seized by Chinese police in the Harbin Consulate left no doubt on this point. Russian denials carried no conviction to Japanese minds, and the fact that Chang Hsueh-liang had to fight alone against Soviet armed forces indicated that Chiang-Kai-shek was either too weak to guard the frontiers of Manchuria effectively or was not deeply disturbed by the Russian chastisement of the war lord of the Three Eastern Provinces. The Japanese bastions of defense in North China were in evident danger.

This fact seemed apparent to Japanese statesmen when they looked at the ominous failure of Chiang Kai-shek to cope with communist armies. In December 1930, Chiang mobilized troops, from Hunan, Hopeh, and Kiangsi provinces and sent them against the Communists. The Reds soon annihilated the Eighteenth Corps under General Chang Hueitsan and caused the rapid retreat of the Fiftieth Corps. In February 1931, General Ho Ying-chin was given three army corps to attack the Reds but by May his forces were compelled to withdraw. In July, Chiang Kai-shek himself led a large army to the Nanchang front but accomplished nothing decisive.[33] The Red menace was daily becoming more formidable and Japanese fears rapidly increased. The only way to insure Japanese security was through adequate measures of defense in Manchuria. These might violate some shadowy rights of sovereignty that China had over Manchuria, but these rights had not been successfully asserted since 1912 and would soon

[30] Ambassador Hanihara to Secretary Hughes, April 10, 1924. 711.945/1043, MS, Department of State.

[31] Ambassador Hanihara to Secretary Hughes, April 17, 1924. 711.945/1051, MS, Department of State. President Coolidge signed the Exclusion Act on May 26, 1924.

[32] Secretary Hughes to Senator Lodge, April 17, 1924. Calvin Coolidge MS, Library of Congress.

[33] *Communism in China, Document A, Appendix No. 3* (Tokyo, 1932), pp. 3–5. This document was published by the Japanese Government as a part of the case of Japan. For a sympathetic account of the struggle of Chiang Kai-shek with the Chinese Communists see T'ang Leang-Li, *Suppressing Communist Banditry in China* (Shanghai, 1934), chap. 5.

be extinguished by Russia if Japan took no action. For Japan, expansion in Manchuria was a national imperative. . . .

To Japan it appeared obvious that Manchuria was essential to her as a bastion of defense and as the keystone of her economic structure. Her statesmen hoped that the Department of State would recognize that North China was just as important to Japan as the Caribbean area was to the United States. The American Government had sent military forces to Haiti and to the Dominican Republic for the purpose of establishing administrations that would be responsive to American desires.[34] This armed intervention had been so recent and so effective that it led the American chargé in Peking to send a dispatch to Secretary Kellogg which ended on a significant note: "We cannot oppose Japanese plans in Manchuria ethically in view of measures we have taken in our correspondingly vital zone — the Caribbean."[35] . . .

THE MURDER OF CAPTAIN NAKAMURA. In the hostile atmosphere that had developed in the summer of 1931 it required merely a spark to start an explosion. This spark was provided by the murder of Captain Nakamura on June 27, 1931. The captain, accompanied by three interpreters and assistants, was sent into Manchuria, during the summer of 1931, on a military mission. At Harbin, where his passport was examined by Chinese authorities, he represented himself as an agricultural expert. After proceeding some distance on the Chinese Eastern Railway, he was "placed under detention by Chinese soldiers under Kuan Yuheng, the Commander of the Third

Regiment of the Reclamation Army." On June 27 he and his companions "were shot by Chinese soldiers and their bodies were cremated to conceal evidence of the deed."[36]

The Japanese insisted that the

killing of Captain Nakamura and his companions was unjustified and showed arrogant disrespect for the Japanese Army and nation; they asserted that the Chinese authorities in Manchuria delayed to institute official enquiries into the circumstances, were reluctant to assume responsibility for the occurrence, and were insincere in their claim that they were making every effort to ascertain the facts in the case.[37]

It is certainly true that long delays did occur in trying to "ascertain the facts in the case," and there is no doubt that they "put a severe strain on the patience of the Japanese." It is also true that this Nakamura case, "more than any other single incident, greatly aggravated the resentment of the Japanese and their agitation in favour of forceful means to effect a solution of outstanding Sino-Japanese difficulties in regard to Manchuria."[38]

While the Lytton Commission was studying the situation in China, it noted with concern the increasing strength of communism. In 1930 armies of the Nationalist Government had been unsuccessful in operations against communist forces, and during the following year Chiang Kai-shek was reported to be driving the Communists back in full retreat towards Fukien when the Mukden Incident occurred. But they were elusive and resourceful antagonists. During the

[34] Hallett Abend, *New York Times,* November 4, 1931.

[35] Ferdinand L. Mayer to Secretary Kellogg, Peking, November 22, 1927. 894.51 So 8/4, MS, Department of State.

[36] *Report of the Commission of Enquiry Appointed by the League of Nations on Manchuria* (Washington, 1932) (hereafter referred to as the *Lytton Report*), pp. 63–64.

[37] *Ibid.,* p. 64.

[38] *Ibid.,* p. 65.

autumn of 1931 they resumed their offensive and soon "large parts of the provinces of Fukien and Kiangsi, and parts of Kwantung were reliably reported to be completely sovietized."[39]

Japan was well aware of the danger that this Red tide might roll over most of China. In the documents presented to the Lytton Commission in 1932, emphasis was placed upon this communist menace and upon the apparent inability of the Chinese Nationalist Government to control it.[40] It seemed to Tokyo that Japanese interests in North China were about to be crushed between the millstones of Chinese nationalism and Russian bolshevism. An appeal to the League of Nations would accomplish little. Chinese nationalism had found a sympathetic audience in the Western powers. Most of them were inclined to accept the fictions and pretensions put forward by the Nanking Government. The Japanese position in North China was in grave danger of being infiltrated by Reds or successfully attacked by fervent Chinese Nationalists whose patriotism had turned into a "flame of hatred."[41]

The dilemma that faced Japan is clearly and cogently stated by George Sokolsky who was used as an intermediary between China and Japan in 1931:

It needs to be recalled here that in 1931 the last efforts were made to reconcile these countries [China and Japan]. Actually, I was an instrument in that attempted reconciliation, going to Japan from China to hold meetings with Baron Shidehara, Minister of Foreign Affairs, and others. I can say that the Japanese attitude was conciliatory; the Chinese, on the whole, antagonistic. . . . Two forces were at work to keep China and Japan

quarreling: Soviet Russia and the League of Nations. Soviet Russia had been engaged since 1924 in an active program of stirring hate among the Chinese people against all foreigners except the Russians, but particularly against the British and the Japanese. The League of Nations secretariat was developing in China a field of widespread activity through its agent, Dr. Ludwic Rajchmann, who was spending most of his time in China. Rajchmann was violently anti-Japanese, although Japan was a member of the League of Nations and Rajchmann an employee. Rajchmann is a Pole and is now associated with the United Nations.[42]

Secretary Stimson Prepares a Path to War

One of the reasons why Japan was "conciliatory" towards China in 1931 was because of the shaky structure of Japanese finance. A war with China might lead to very serious consequences. On September 18, 1931, the American press published a summary of a report made by Dr. Harold G. Moulton, of the Brookings Institution, on economic conditions in the Japanese Empire. This survey had been undertaken upon the invitation of the Japanese Minister of Finance. In conclusion the summary stated that "military retrenchment, continuation of peaceful relations with the United States, and sharp restriction of the present rates of population are all essential if serious economic and financial difficulties in Japan are to be averted. . . . A balanced budget and tax reduction can be accomplished only if military outlays are curtailed."[43]

It was only with the greatest reluctance, therefore, that Japanese statesmen consented to support a program of expansion in Manchuria. After it was apparent that the Japanese Kwantung Army had seized certain cities in North

[39] Ibid., p. 22.

[40] Communism in China, Document A, Appendix No. 3 (Tokyo, 1932).

[41] Lytton Report, op. cit., p. 19.

[42] George Sokolsky, "These Days," Washington Times-Herald, March 14, 1951.

[43] Ware, op. cit., p. 206.

China, Hugh Byas, writing from Tokyo, reported that the sudden movement of troops had not been "foreseen" by the Japanese Government and had not been preventable.[44] Byas, as well as many other veteran observers in the Far East, had great confidence in the pacific disposition of Baron Shidehara, the Japanese Minister of Foreign Relations. Secretary Stimson shared this view and at first he was anxious to refrain from exerting too much pressure upon the Japanese Government because he feared such a policy would play into the hands of the militarists. . . .

The bombing of Chinchow by Japanese planes on October 8 provoked Stimson to take more vigorous action to preserve peace. He now began to consider the employment of sanctions against Japan in order to compel her to "respect the great peace treaties."[45] On October 10 he secured the President's approval of a suggestion to have an American representative participate in all the sessions of the League Council which dealt with the enforcement of the Kellogg-Briand Pact. . . .

On October 17, with Mr. Gilbert in attendance, the Council of the League decided upon a joint invocation of the Kellogg-Briand Pact. After Stimson had been assured that the League would take action he sent (October 20) identic notes to China and Japan reminding them of their obligations under the pact.[46] The Council took the further step (October 24) of calling upon Japan to "begin immediately with the withdrawal of its troops into the railway zone" of the

South Manchuria Railway. This withdrawal should be completed by November 16.[47]

Edwin Neville, the American chargé at Tokyo, regarded this directive of the League as inopportune and ineffective and he requested the Department of State to refrain from giving it any support. American co-operation in this particular case would "weaken American influence in Japan" and would not "accomplish anything" in settling the Manchurian dispute.[48]

Stimson paid scant attention to this advice. On November 5, Ambassador Forbes handed to the Japanese Foreign Minister a memorandum which closely followed the phraseology of the League resolution with the exception that no time limit was set for the withdrawal of the Japanese troops.[49] On November 19 he fired another shot in this barrage against Japan. In a conversation with Debuchi he warned him that the American Government might publish the diplomatic correspondence that had passed between the Foreign Office and the Department of State and thus mobilize world opoinion against the actions of Japanese militarists.[50]

After this thrust against Japan, Stimson once more turned to the League and explained the basis of American action. Pressure from President Hoover had softened the tone of his notes. When Stimson in Cabinet meetings began to

[44] *New York Times,* September 19, 1931.

[45] Henry L. Stimson, *The Far Eastern Crisis: Recollections and Observations* (New York, 1936), pp. 51–57.

[46] Secretary Stimson to the American Minister in China and to the American chargé d'affaires in Japan, October 20, 1931. *Ibid.,* p. 275.

[47] *Foreign Relations: Japan, 1931–1941,* I, 29–30.

[48] Chargé in Japan (Neville) to Secretary Stimson, Tokyo, November 4, 1931. *Foreign Relations, 1931,* III, 366–67.

[49] Memorandum of a conversation between Ambassador Forbes (Tokyo) with the Japanese Minister for Foreign Affairs (Shidehara), November 5, 1931. *Ibid.,* pp. 375–80.

[50] Memorandum by the Secretary of State of a conversation with the Japanese Ambassador (Debuchi), November 19, 1931. *Foreign Relations: Japan, 1931–1941,* I, 44–46.

talk about coercing Japan by all "means short of actual use of armed force," the President informed him that "this was simply the road to war itself and he would have none of it."[51]

Stimson, therefore, instructed Ambassador Dawes to tell certain members of the League Council that, while the American fleet would not take any adverse action against any embargo that would be enforced against Japanese commerce, it should be clearly understood that the United States would not participate in any economic sanctions. America would assist in mobilizing public opinion against Japan and would refuse to recognize "any treaties that were created under military force."[52]

Under the impact of this American pressure, Shidehara desperately strove to modify the policy of the militarists in Tokyo and on November 27 he was able to put a brief stop to the Manchurian advance. But the Japanese Cabinet fell two weeks later and these futile peace gestures ceased. On January 2, 1932, Chinchow was captured and the Japanese conquestion of Manchuria was complete.

Before this took place Elihu Root, thoroughly alarmed by the active measures Secretary Stimson was taking to stop Japanese expansion in Manchuria, wrote the Secretary a long letter of protest. Root had been Secretary of State from 1905 to 1909 and had negotiated the Root-Takahira Agreement that had given Japan a green light in Manchuria. He now warned Stimson about "getting entangled in League measures which we

have no right to engage in against Japan." He also alluded to Japan's special interests in Manchuria through a long period of years, and spoke of the need for Japan to protect herself in a political sense against "the dagger aimed at her heart."

Root was a realist who did not want war with Japan. Stimson was a pacifist who loved peace so much he was always ready to fight for it. He wholeheartedly subscribed to the slogan — perpetual war for perpetual peace. In his answer to Root he expressed the belief that his intervention in the Manchurian muddle was necessary to save the whole structure of the peace treaties. He was the Atlas on whose stooping shoulders world peace was precariously balanced. A "new advance by Japan" would "undoubtedly create much adverse and even hostile sentiment in this country and much pressure upon us for some kind of action." As a man of action he was not inclined to draw back into any shell of neutrality.[53] . . .

For the next two months Stimson had to stand responsible for the nonrecognition policy without any help from Great Britain, but there were certain factors that slowly pushed the Foreign Office into line with the Department of State. Britain had extensive business interests in Shanghai, and when the Japanese, on January 28, 1932, opened an offensive against the Chinese Nineteenth Route Army stationed in that city, the situation took on a new aspect.

. . . Time and British big business were working on his side. On February 16 the League Council sent an appeal to Japan for the purpose of dissuading her from making a full-scale attack upon Shanghai. In this appeal Japan was pointed out as the responsible party in

[51] Ray L. Wilbur and Arthur M. Hyde, *The Hoover Policies* (New York, 1937), p. 603.

[52] Memorandum of a trans-Atlantic telephone conversation between Secretary Stimson and Ambassador Dawes, November 19, 1931. *Foreign Relations, 1931*, III, 488–98.

[53] Secretary Stimson to Elihu Root, December 14, 1931, Strictly Personal and Confidential, Box 129, Root Papers, Library of Congress.

the Far Eastern conflict, and she was reminded of her obligations under the Covenant of the League of Nations and under the provisions of the Nine-Power Treaty.[54] On March 11 the Assembly of the League took a bolder step when it adopted a resolution which declared that it was "incumbent upon the members of the League of Nations not to recognize any situation, treaty or agreement which may be brought about by means contrary to the Covenant of the League of Nations or to the Pact of Paris."[55]

Secretary Stimson had at last maneuvered the League of Nations into a formal approval of the nonrecognition theory. It was a fateful step along a "dead-end" street of fear and frustration, and its inevitable consequence was America's involvement in World War II.[56]

SECRETARY STIMSON PRODUCES A PATTERN OF WAR

As one means of coping with the Japanese advance in North China, Stimson sent Joseph C. Grew to Tokyo as the American Ambassador. When Grew arrived in Japan in June 1932, the press was friendly and the Emperor was as agreeable as Mr. Grew's deafness permitted him to be. But the shadows of the Manchurian adventure fell across the threshold of the American Embassy and Grew soon realized that they would probably deepen and lengthen despite all his efforts to banish them with the bright light of some new Japanese-American understanding.

The main barrier across the road to friendly relations was the Stimson doctrine itself. The Japanese Government was determined to recognize Manchukuo in defiance of adverse opinion in the United States and in Europe. Secure control over North China appeared to Japanese statesmen, regardless of party affiliations, as a national necessity. As a source of essential raw materials and as a market for manufactured goods, Manchuria had special importance for Japan. Presidents Theodore Roosevelt and Woodrow Wilson had been willing to regard certain portions of North China as a Japanese sphere of influence, and the language of the Root-Takahira and the Lansing-Ishii agreements was so vaguely fertile that Japanese aspirations had enjoyed a rapid growth. Theodore Roosevelt, after boldly plucking the Pan-

[54] Irving S. Friedman, *British Relations with China, 1931–1939* (New York, 1940), p. 33.

[55] The consul at Geneva (Gilbert) to Secretary Stimson, Geneva, March 15, 1932. *Foreign Relations, 1932*, III, 585–86. Westel W. Willoughby, *The Sino-Japanese Controversy and the League of Nations* (Baltimore, 1935), pp. 299–301.

[56] The dangers that were inherent in the Far Eastern situation were discussed at length by the British Prime Minister (Ramsay MacDonald) in a conversation with Mr. Atherton, the American chargé d'affaires at London, on April 4, 1932: "In substance the Prime Minister said that it was foreseen some time ago by critics of the League that members might well be actually in a state of war without a formal declaration of war, in order to escape the penalties placed upon war by the Covenant. This was in fact what had happened in the present instance, although the Chinese had almost 'put the fat in the fire.' During the last Far Eastern discussions in Geneva the Chinese had drawn up a resolution which a League representative agreed formally to present. This resolution declared that Japan by her actions was in fact in a state of war with members of the League.

"The League representative showed this resolution to Sir John Simon who said that he would have nothing to do with it and that if it were presented he would deny all knowledge of it. Eventually the resolution just escaped presentation, but the Prime Minister said that this showed how near Japan had been to open conflict with members of the League." 793.94/4965. *Confidential file*, MS, Department of State.

ama pear, could not turn a deaf ear to Japanese pleas for a bite of Manchurian melon. And Woodrow Wilson, deep in his preparations for a crusade against wicked Germany, could not look too closely into Japanese motives in Manchuria. Encouraged by these friendly gestures of American Presidents, Japanese armies moved into many parts of North China. When Stimson suddenly flashed a red light of warning against any further advance, the Japanese Government made no real effort to obey the signal. Their Manchurian machine had gained too much momentum to be stopped by an American traffic cop who merely blew a tin whistle of non-recognition.

The efforts of European statesmen were just as futile as those of Secretary Stimson. The Lytton Commission, appointed under the terms of the League resolution of December 10, 1931, reached Tokyo on February 29, 1932, for a series of conferences with Japanese statesmen and with representatives of various Japanese organizations. From April 20 to June 4 the commission took testimony in Manchuria, and then returned to Tokyo for a brief sojourn. It finally moved to Peiping to complete the task of drafting a formal report.

While the commission was in Tokyo, Major General Frank R. McCoy talked freely to Ambassador Grew. He assured the ambassador that the commission was of the opinion that Japan's action in Manchuria was based on two false premises: the argument of self-defense and the argument of self-determination. The commission was also convinced that the erection of a puppet state like Manchukuo "would result in a festering sore which will inevitably lead to future wars." Although Mr. Grew shared these viewpoints, he warned Secretary Stimson that any pro-

test from the United States concerning Japanese recognition of Manchukuo would play right into the hands of the military clique in Tokyo. Silence would pay good diplomatic dividends.[57]

But the task of silencing Stimson was as difficult as stopping the rush of waters over Niagara Falls. He was so full of righteous indignation that he had to deliver a new blast against Japan on August 8 in an address before the Council on Foreign Relations (New York City). As Grew had anticipated, the reaction in Japan to this latest Stimson attack was widespread and bitter. Its violence caused Grew to warn Stimson that "we should have our eyes open to all possible future contingencies."[58] The policy of constantly pricking Japan might eventually lead to a dangerous outburst.

On September 3, Grew sent another telegram of warning. The Japanese Government firmly intended to see "the Manchuria venture through." The Japanese public was convinced that the "whole course of action in Manchuria is one of supreme and vital national interest," and it was determined to meet, if necessary with arms, "all opposition."[59] After sending this telegram to the Department of State, Grew confided to his *Diary* that Japanese resentment was really focused upon only one American — Secretary Stimson. Everyone he met in Japan was

[57] Ambassador Grew to Secretary Stimson, Tokyo, July 16, 1932. *Foreign Relations: Japan, 1931–1941*, I, 93–95. On June 21, 1932, Viscount Ishii had made a speech before the America-Japan Society of Tokyo in which he gave assurances that Japan would leave "no stone unturned in order to remove all possible causes of friction with her great neighbor." Shanghai *Evening Post and Mercury*, June 21, 1932.

[58] Ambassador Grew to Secretary Stimson, Tokyo, August 13, 1932. *Foreign Relations: Japan, 1931–1941*, I, 100.

[59] Ambassador Grew to Secretary Stimson, Tokyo, September 3, 1932. *Ibid.*, p. 102.

"thoroughly friendly" and his personal relations with Japanese officials were of "the best." But Stimson had enraged all Japan with his policy of constant hostile pressure.[60] It was not hard for a diplomat to see the inevitable result of these tactics.

In some circles in Japan the hope was expressed that a change in the Administration in Washington would bring a change in Far Eastern policy. But Stimson still had some six months to serve as Secretary of State, and there was the ominous possibility that during the period he would so firmly fix the pattern of policy that a new Secretary would be unable to alter it. Of one thing everyone in Japan could be certain — Stimson would not recede from the stand he had taken, no matter what the result. America might not be pushed to the point of actual conflict with Japan, but the road to war would be wide open and an invitation to hostilities would be ready for the anxious consideration of the President-elect.

In order to make sure that this invitation would be no empty affair, Stimson had consented to have Major General Frank R. McCoy serve as a member of the Lytton Commission of Enquiry. If this commission denounced Japanese aggression in North China in acidulous terms, General McCoy would bear a portion of the responsibility for such an indictment.

On October 1, 1932, the report of the Lytton Commission was published in Geneva. It made some interesting admissions. The rapid growth of the Communist Party was briefly described and the inability of Chiang Kai-shek to suppress it was clearly indicated.[61] But nothing was said about Soviet infiltration of Sinkiang and the absorption of Outer Mongolia. Japan was to be the culprit in China, not Russia. In order to prove this point the report expressed in very positive terms the belief that Japan made use of the Mukden Incident of September 18 to carry out a far-reaching plan of expansion in North China. It was admitted that Japan had "special interests" in Manchuria but these interests did not justify the erection of a semi-independent state like Manchukuo which would be under Japanese control. The report therefore recommended that Manchuria should enjoy "a large measure of autonomy" consistent "with the sovereignty and administrative integrity of China."[62]

The report mentioned the fact that the Japanese had erected the new state of Manchukuo on March 9, 1932, and had installed Henry Pu-yi, the boy Emperor of China, as the regent. It did not indicate who was to dethrone the regent or who was to assume the grave responsibility of pushing the large Japanese Army out of Manchukuo and thus permit Manchuria to resume its former status. Indirectly, this assertion of continued Chinese sovereignty over the Three Provinces was an endorsement of the Stimson nonrecognition principle. The commission conveniently closed its eyes to the fact of Japanese control over Manchukuo and assumed that the farce of nonrecognition would bring Japan to heel. It was a little shocked when Japan formally recognized Manchukuo on September 15, and Secretary Stimson felt outraged at this defiance of his doctrine.

Two months later (November 19) Matsuoka, the head of the Japanese delegation at Geneva, whispered some warn-

---

[60] Joseph C. Grew, *Ten Years in Japan* (New York, 1944), p. 40.

[61] *Lytton Report* (Washington, 1932), pp. 20–23.

[62] *Ibid.*, p. 130.

ing words to Hugh Wilson and Norman Davis. The hostility of the Japanese public toward the United States was "dangerous." There was a growing belief that several attempts had been made by the American Government to "check Japanese development in Manchuria and to get control of the railway situation in that area." The large body of influential Japanese opinion that heretofore had been friendly was "rapidly diminishing." The Japanese people had been very patient, but a point had been reached where this quality was no longer a virtue and the repressed irritation against America might break through all bonds with "suddenness and violence."[63]

Matsuoka had spent many years in the United States as a student and was known among the Japanese as "thinking and conducting himself like an American."[64] His words of warning would have had some influence upon the average Secretary of State, but Stimson refused to heed them. He carelessly boasted to Hugh Wilson that he was acquainted with the "personality and methods" of Matsuoka and had anticipated that he would assume the airs of a "clever advocate."[65] If Stimson had been blest with a more perceptive mind, he would have realized that Matsuoka was not indulging in idle threats. His words were freighted with wisdom, but Stimson still clung to the idea that he could beat the Japanese Foreign Minister into submission with the club of nonrecognition. It gave him small concern if the Foreign Minister squirmed under this punishment

and if the Japanese press grew violent in its denunciations of his policy. The Japanese would have to take their medicine no matter how bitter it tasted. . . .

In the meantime the League of Nations was giving extended consideration to the implications of the Lytton Report. On December 6 the League Assembly referred the report to a Committee of Nineteen. The representatives of several small nations on this committee were profoundly provoked with Japan because of her military operations in Manchuria. They made up for their military weakness in cascades of strong words of criticism. Stimson's quick ear caught these caustic accents and he repeated them to the Japanese Ambassador. On January 5, 1933, he talked with Debuchi, and after reviewing Japanese disregard of certain treaty obligations, he acidly observed that really there was "no other course" for Japan to follow but "to get out of the League of Nations and the Kellogg Pact.[66]

After reading this stiff lecture to the Japanese Ambassador, Stimson found time to visit Hyde Park on January 9 where he found President-elect Roosevelt in a very receptive mood. He had no trouble in convincing Roosevelt that the Stimson doctrine should be one of the pillars of the foreign policy of the new Administration. Three days later he informed Ambassador Debuchi that the President-elect would adhere to the Stimson policy.[67] On January 16 this news was sent to our diplomatic representatives abroad, and on the following day Roosevelt, at a press conference at Hyde

[63] Secretary Stimson to Ambassador Grew, Washington, November 21, 1932. *Japan and the United States: 1931–1941*, I, 104–5.

[64] Frederick Moore, *With Japan's Leaders* (New York, 1942), pp. 130–31.

[65] Secretary Stimson to Hugh Wilson, November 21, 1932. *Japan and the United States, 1931–1941*, I, 105.

[66] Conversation between Secretary Stimson and Ambassador Debuchi, January 5, 1933. 793.94/5709, *Confidential file*, MS, Department of State.

[67] Conversation between Secretary Stimson and Ambassador Debuchi, January 12, 1933. *Japan and the United States, 1931–1941*, I, 108–9.

Park, insisted that America must stand behind the principle of the "sanctity of treaties."[68] Party lines in America had disappeared when it came to imposing discipline upon Japan. . . .

Even if Secretary Stimson had been sincere in his desire to make some gesture of conciliation towards Japan, it was apparent that time was against him. In a few weeks the Roosevelt Administration would take office and it would be most unusual for an outgoing Secretary of State to take a major diplomatic step which might not be in complete agreement with the policy already outlined by his successor in office after March 4, 1933. At any rate Stimson did nothing to conciliate Japanese statesmen who were now determined to take some radical action at Geneva. The Roosevelt statement at Hyde Park on January 17 in favor of the "sanctity of treaties" failed to make much of an impression upon them. They knew that the British and French empires had been built by the blood, sweat, and tears of millions of persons in conquered countries. Why all this sudden show of international virtue? As Matsuoka sagely remarked: "The Western Powers taught the Japanese the game of poker but after acquiring most of the chips they pronounced the game immoral and took up contract bridge."[69] It was obvious to most Japanese statesmen that the conscience of the Western powers barked only at strangers.

Matsuoka Marches Out of the League

At Geneva, Matsuoka was not inclined to listen to lectures in the League Assembly on public morals, and Ambassador Grew on February 23, 1933, informed Secretary Stimson that the Japanese Cabinet was in entire agreement with the viewpoint of their chief delegate. They regarded their position in Manchuria as an essential link in the "life line" of the Japanese Empire. They were determined to fight rather than yield to League pressure.[70] In the face of this resolute Japanese attitude, the League went ahead and on February 24 it formally approved by an overwhelming vote the report of the Committee of Nineteen which had implemented the Lytton Report.[71]

This critical action on the part of the Assembly of the League of Nations provoked an immediate response from Matsuoka. After gravely stating that his government had "reached the limit of its endeavors to co-operate with the League," he marched stiffly from the hall of the Assembly. . . .

Hugh Wilson, representing the United States, was also in the Assembly as Matsuoka walked out. Like Frederick Moore he also realized that a crisis had been reached in world politics, and this crisis he knew had been precipitated by Stimson's nonrecognition policy. In his memoirs, Wilson tells the story of that fateful march of Matsuoka:

The final session of the Assembly remains indelibly printed on my mind. . . . Matsuoka's speech on that day in the Assembly was delivered with a passionate conviction far removed from his usual businesslike manner.

[68] *New York Times,* January 18, 1933. Stimson had already assured the British Foreign Secretary, Sir John Simon, that the President-elect was committed to the Stimson doctrine. Sir John replied, January 14, that the British Government would adhere to the same doctrine. *Foreign Relations, 1933,* III, 89.

[69] Moore, *op. cit.,* pp. 38–39.

[70] *Japan and the United States: 1931–1941,* I, 110–12. On February 7, 1933, with his tongue in his cheek, Stimson instructed Hugh Wilson, United States Minister at Geneva, to make it clear that he was not in any way attempting "to guide or to influence or prejudice the League in its deliberations." *Foreign Relations, 1933,* III, 153.

[71] Russell M. Cooper, *American Consultation in World Affairs,* pp. 268–69.

He pointed out the danger of pillorying a great nation. He warned that the Assembly was driving Japan from its friendship with the West toward an inevitable development of a self-sustaining, uniquely Eastern position. . . . For the first time the gravest doubts arose as to the wisdom of the course which the Assembly and my country were pursuing. I began to have a conception of the rancor and resentment that public condemnation could bring upon a proud and powerful people, and I began to question, and still do question whether such treatment is wise. . . . Condemnation creates a community of the damned who are forced outside the pale, who have nothing to lose by the violation of all laws of order and international good faith. . . . Not only did such doubts regarding arraignment arise in me, but for the first time I began to question the non-recognition policy. More and more as I thought it over I became conscious that we had entered a dead-end street.[72]

It was apparent to seasoned diplomats that the manner in which Stimson endeavored to apply the nonrecognition formula was so provocative that war and not peace would be the result of his efforts. The world was not ready to purchase future peace at the price of immediate war. In Tokyo, Ambassador Grew became increasingly dubious with regard to the frenzied actions of Stimson to stop the Japanese advance into Manchuria. It seemed to him that the "peace machinery which the world has been trying . . . to erect these last fourteen years" was basically "unsound." How could statesmen really expect to halt the tides of national ambition by the paper dykes of peace treaties like the Pact of Paris? Could such a pact have stopped the movement that pushed America into conflict with Spain in 1898? Moral sanctions would have little effect upon nations that

had completed their blueprints for plunder. And if moral ostracism were "ineffective," how could America "implement the Kellogg Pact?" Certainly not by the force of arms which would be "contrary to the very principle for which the Kellogg Pact stands." Neither the severance of diplomatic relations nor the imposition of economic boycotts would check nations that were moving down the broad highway to war. The future peace of the world could be preserved only by removing the causes of conflict and not by trying to restrict its scope or to soften its impact.[73]

At the same time that Ambassador Grew was recording in his diary these sapient observations, he was writing a dispatch to Secretary Stimson in a very different vein. Japan was essentially a wicked nation with no real understanding of moral obligations. This being so it "would seem that the world was hardly justified in taking for granted that Japan would observe the letter and spirit of international agreements." This "callous disregard of the pledged word" was the "growth of centuries" and could be traced to the fact that in Japan "there was nothing to correspond to the rules of abstract justice contained in the old Roman law." As a result of this lack of knowledge of Roman law the "Japanese naturally do not look upon contracts and agreements as do Occidental peoples."[74]

While Mr. Grew was writing this critical commentary upon the "unmoral" Japanese, his counselor of Embassy, Mr. Neville, was writing an equally caustic memorandum upon the faithless Chinese. It was apparent to him that the Chinese

---

[72] Hugh R. Wilson, *Diplomat Between Wars* (New York, 1941), pp. 279–81.

[73] Grew *Diary*, February 23, 1933; *Ten Years in Japan*, pp. 78–80.

[74] Ambassador Grew to Secretary Stimson, February 21, 1933. 793.94/6026, MS, Department of State.

Government had failed to carry out many of the engagements undertaken at the Washington Conference of 1921–22. Moreover, the menace of Red Russia was growing more formidable every day:

In this atmosphere of distrust and suspicion, aggravated by the world-wide economic collapse and internal problems of industrial and social discontent, the Japanese looked about them. In addition to the normal difficulties in China, the Japanese were subjected to an intense boycott; the situation in Manchuria appeared worse than ever as the Chinese had used borrowed money to operate railways to the detriment of the Japanese line; their various agreements with the Chinese remained unimplemented and in the background was Soviet Russia, apparently once more a Power. The Washington undertakings were unfulfilled, and the Conference called to supplement the Naval Treaty had ignored the actual conditions that Japan had to face. So in 1931 Japan acted alone. . . . The British had acted alone in Shanghai and the British and Americans had acted together at Nanking in 1927. . . . After the Japanese action in September, 1931, the Chinese appealed to the League of Nations, alleging aggression on the part of Japan and asking redress under the Covenant. . . . The Chinese are in no position to bring up any of the Washington settlements. They have defaulted on their obligations thereunder and do not come into court with clean hands.[75]

Secretary Stimson would not have agreed with this indictment of the government of China, and the Division of Far Eastern Affairs continued to needle Japan. On his way home from the debacle at Geneva, Matsuoka passed through the United States and hoped to have a conference with President Roosevelt. When this news came to the Department of

State, Mr. Hornbeck immediately wrote a memorandum indicating that it "would be undesirable to have the new President grant Mr. Matsuoka an interview." If he (Matsuoka) were "to speak with the President it would be only natural for the public to assume that Matsuoka had endeavored to convince the President of the justice of the Japanese case."[76] For some reason that is not clear, Mr. Hornbeck believed that the American public should not be placed under the strain of having to follow the arguments of Matsuoka. There was a chance that they might be too cogent and thus defeat the repressive policy of the Department of State. As a result of Mr. Hornbeck's advice, Matsuoka did not have an opportunity to present in private the case of Japan relative to Manchukuo.

While the Department of State was striving to check any conciliatory gestures in the direction of Japan, the student body of Meiji University, in Tokyo, was extending to the President-elect their "heartfelt congratulations" upon his election: "The fact that our Japanese public rejoiced over your victory, we believe is a clear evidence of the great significance we are placing upon your Administration. . . . We hope that you will reweigh the Manchurian troubles and try and comprehend that the cause is not so simple as one might think."[77]

[75] Ambassador Grew to Secretary Stimson, Tokyo, February 24, 1933, with inclosure by Mr. Neville, counselor of the Embassy. 793.94/6031, MS, Department of State.

[76] Memorandum by Mr. Hornbeck, Division of Far Eastern Affairs, February 28, 1933. 811.4611 Japan/24, MS, Department of State. On March 31, 1933, Matsuoka had a brief interview with Secretary Hull. He was "very affable" and "urged that Japan be given time in which to make herself better understood." With reference to this conversation, Mr. Hull remarks: "I was courteous but virtually silent while he was offering these parting remarks." *Foreign Relations, 1933*, p. 264.

[77] Memorial from the editorial staff of the *Sundai Shimpo*, student publication of Meiji University, Tokyo, Japan, to President Roosevelt, February 22, 1933. 711.94/792, MS, Department of State.

The Japanese press also expressed an ardent desire that the Roosevelt Administration would take an understanding view of the Manchurian situation and thereby lay the basis for "a restoration of friendly relations between the two nations." Matsuoka himself was quite optimistic with reference to Japanese-American relations. He thought that all talk of war between the two countries was "ridiculous." If Japan went to war in the near future, it would be with Soviet Russia, and Matsuoka expressed the view that in that event "he would not be surprised to see the United States on Japan's side."

There was no doubt that Japan had no wish for a war with the United States. Matsuoka was correct in his belief that the logical opponent for Japan in her next war would be Russia, but logic was not the basis for the foreign policy of the Roosevelt Administration. The wish that was closest to Stalin's heart was to involve Japan and the United States in a war that would remove the Japanese barrier that prevented the Red tide from overflowing the wide plains of China. The way that wish was gratified is the story of the succeeding chapters on Japanese-American relations. . . .

Japan Promotes Autonomy Movement in North China

It had been very clear to Theodore Roosevelt during his administration as President that Japan regarded Manchuria as a bulwark of defense and as the keystone in the economic structure of the empire. Japan could not retire from her position in that province and any attempt to force her withdrawal would lead to open warfare. President Franklin D. Roosevelt and Secretary Hull by adopting the Stimson formula of nonrecognition had opened a Pandora's box of troubles in the Far East. When they applied the formula to Japan and remained silent concerning Russa's absorption of Outer Mongolia, they emptied every evil in the box and led them to stalk along the Manchurian frontier stirring up discontent.

Chaos and communism are close companions and as Japan looked over the unsettled condition of affairs in North China, it was apparent that Russian agents were busily at work in fomenting discord. They would turn the peasants against the tottering regime of Chiang Kai-shek, and when the fires of revolution had destroyed the weak fabric of the Nationalist Government, communist armies under Mao Tse-tung or Chu Teh would quickly extinguish them under a heavy iron curtain. The formula was simple and very effective. If Japan remained inactive in North China, it would not be long before Manchuria and Korea would be closely besieged by great masses of fanatical Reds. Japan must either extend her frontiers in China or see her troops pushed into the sea.

Soviet Russia Promotes a War between China and Japan

It is apparent from the diplomatic correspondence that came to the Department of State from Nanking and Tokyo that in the summer of 1937 many Chinese officials were spoiling for a fight between Japan and China. In June 1937, Mr. Andrews, second secretary of the American Embassy in Tokyo, had a conversation with Dr. Mar who held a similar position in the Chinese Embassy. After Ambassador Grew read a report of this conversation he noted that Dr. Mar's attitude was "one of truculence and undue optimism, thus reflecting the enhanced sense of security that has been developed in a section of Chinese officialdom as a consequence of the development of the past year."[78] China, and not Japan, was ready for the outbreak of hostilities.

In China the Japanese Ambassador kept speaking in a conciliatory vein which stressed the idea that "the time would come when there would be 'understandings' between China and Japan." As a result of these pacific words Mr. Gauss, the American Consul-General at Shanghai, reported that in informed quarters it was believed that "the Japanese are unlikely to display a strong attitude or to take any aggressive measures in North China while the question of an Anglo-Japanese understanding is being explored."[79]

It is evident that many foreign observers in June–July 1937 regarded an outbreak of war between China and Japan as quite improbable. The Konoye Ministry seemed intent upon carrying out the pacific policy of the preceding adminis-

trations. It was with distinct surprise, therefore, that the governments of the major powers heard that armed hostilities had taken place near Peiping. On the night of July 7, in the vicinity of the famous Marco Polo bridge, some Japanese troops became involved in a sharp fight with some units of the Chinese Twenty-ninth Army.[80] A new drama that would end on a curtain line announcing Russian domination of the Far East had opened with an ominous fanfare. The whole world became an interested audience with few of the spectators realizing that the progress of the play was pointed towards a Russian conclusion. Chinese, Japanese, and Americans would move across the Far Eastern stage in intricate patterns that finally proclaimed a definite Muscovite motif. The Moscow theater never staged a more effective puppet show. . . .

RUSSIA INSTIGATES WAR IN THE FAR EAST; ROOSEVELT BLAMES JAPAN

During the long months that Hitler devoted to redrawing the frontier lines in Europe, Joseph Stalin was preparing to change the map of the Far East. Chiang Kai-shek, as his chief cartographer, would unwittingly splash Red across the chart of eastern Asia all the way from Outer Mongolia to Mukden and then draw back in sudden alarm at the implications of his handiwork. His task could best be done in the atmosphere of armed conflict, and this was produced by Russian agents who blew sparks of friction in North China into the wild

flames of an undeclared Sino-Japanese war.

Communist Instigation of War in the Far East

Communist instigation of the outbreak of the undeclared war of July 7 is indicated in some revealing remarks of the Chinese Ambassador in Moscow. During a conversation with the American diplomatic representative he confessed that he had arrived in Moscow in November 1936 as a "firm supporter of Chinese-

[78] *Ibid.*

[79] C. E. Gauss to Secretary Hull, Shanghai, June 30, 1937. 793.94/8992, MS, Department of State.

[80] Walter H. Mallory, "Japan Attacks, China Resists," *Foreign Affairs*, XVI (October 1937), 129–33; T. A. Bisson, "Origins of Sino-Japanese Hostilities," *Foreign Policy Reports*, XIII (March 1, 1938), 291–300.

Soviet friendship." One of the main purposes of his mission had been "to obtain
assurances from the Soviet Government
that *if China pushed Japan so far as to
make war inevitable, the Soviet Union
would support China with supplies and
armed forces.*"[81] Shortly after his arrival
in Russia he had questioned Litvinov on
this point but had received the answer
that the Soviet Government would prefer
to have this matter settled at Nanking.
In this regard it was significant that during the spring and summer of 1937 the
Russian Ambassador at Nanking had endeavored to "make the Chinese Government believe that if it would undertake
to offer armed resistance to Japan it
could confidently expect the armed support of the Soviet Union."[82]

Communist instigation and continued
support of the conflict between Chinese
and Japanese armed forces in July 1937
were further illustrated by the evident
reluctance of the Kuomintang to agree
to a formula of accommodation. To do
so would mean an open break with the
Communists, who since the Sian agreement, had worked for a common front
between themselves and the Nationalists
against Japan. This situation is well
described in a dispatch from Nanking:

Competent observers here consider the situation as one moving toward war; they point
out that if the National Government should
hold to the former plan of surrendering North
China rather than resist Japanese aggression
there, the National Government's existence
would be seriously jeopardized because it is
believed to have pledged resistance to Japan
as part of the settlement of the Sian revolt
and non-resistance would cause the aliena-

tion of the Communist forces in the north-
west who are about to be incorporated into
the Government's armies.[83]

Japanese military authorities did not
at first appear to realize the strength of
this tie between the Communists and the
Nationalists, and they hoped for an early
settlement of the clash on the night of
July 7. Some of them were inclined to
believe that "the firing by Chinese troops
which started the incident was not pre-
meditated."[84] This conciliatory attitude
led to the agreement of July 11 which
was formally signed by General Chang
on the nineteenth. Its terms were mild.
There would be an apology and some
punishment for the Chinese captain responsible for the outbreak of hostilities.
There would also be assurances for the
future which provided for the voluntary
retirement of Chinese officials in North
China who impeded Sino-Japanese cooperation and the expulsion of the communistic elements from the Peiping
district.[85]

On July 12 the Japanese Ambassador
(Saito) had a long conversation with
Secretary Hull during the course of
which he explained the policy of the
Foreign Office. At the conclusion of
Saito's remarks, Hull expressed his approval of Japanese efforts "to work out
a friendly settlement" of the incident.[86]
On the following day Ambassador Grew
informed the Department of State that
he believed that "if some way of avoiding general hostilities without losing face

[81] The italicizing of this part of the quotation is
the author's.
[82] Mr. Henderson to Secretary Hull, December
21, 1937. 793.94/11763, Moscow, MS, Department of State.

[83] Mr. Peck to Secretary Hull, Nanking, July 12,
1937. 793.94/8715, MS, Department of State.
[84] Walter H. Mallory, "Japan Attacks, China
Resists," *Foreign Affairs*, XVI (1937), 129–33.
[85] Memorandum by the ambassador in Japan
(Grew), Tokyo, July 22, 1937. *United States and
Japan, 1931–1941*, I, 333–34.
[86] Memorandum by Secretary Hull, July 12,
1937. *Ibid.*, pp. 316–18.

could be found, the Japanese Government might possibly still be pleased to find this way."[87]

It seemed to Mr. Hornbeck that the Japanese Foreign Office was taking the position that conversations should not be held by representatives of the Chinese and Japanese governments "but between Japanese officials in North China and the local Chinese officials on the theory that North China is a political entity separate from the authority and control of the Chinese (Nanking) Government." It was his opinion that the American Government should "make no approach to either the Chinese or the Japanese authorities and make no public comment."[88]

Secretary Hull followed this advice. On the evening of July 13 he summoned Ambassador Saito to his apartment in the Carlton Hotel and frankly informed him that the American Government was "paramountly concerned in the preservation of peace." Because of this fact it would confine its utterances "to phases entirely within range of its impartial, friendly attitude towards all alike." Its action would "stop entirely short of any question or phase of mediation."[89]

This "hands off" attitude would continue to be observed by the Department of State if no general war followed the clash at Peiping. In the event of long-continued hostilities tremendous pressure would be exerted upon Secretary Hull to undertake some form of mediation. But in the early days of July 1937 there still seemed some hope for peace. It was true, however, that the action of the Chinese Nationalist Government in disavowing the agreement of July 11 was causing deep concern in the minds of many observers. When this disavowal was followed by the dispatch of "a large body of troops" to the Peiping area, it was obvious that a crisis had arrived.[90] . . .

The British Foreign Office favored a "combined Anglo-American démarche" in Tokyo and Nanking rather than an invocation of the Nine-Power Treaty, and Foreign Secretary Eden suggested this to Ambassador Bingham. From Tokyo, Ambassador Grew expressed a strong dissent from this view. He could see "no reason why we should take action."[91] He also indicated that in Japan the unanimity of opinion relative to the situation in North China was "striking." It was not "a case of unwilling deference by the Government to military initiative. The Cabinet enjoys high prestige, is wholly in command and lends full support to steps recently taken by the Japanese Army in North China. . . . At no time during the period of my assignment at this post have I observed indications of so strong and unanimous a determination on the part of the Japanese Government to resist even at the cost of extensive hostilities any movement which might tend to weaken the position of Japan in North China." Mr. Grew also remarked that there was not sufficient evidence to justify the hypothesis that "either the Japanese Government or the Army deliberately engineered the incident in order to force a 'show down.' "[92] . . .

---

[87] Ambassador Grew to Secretary Hull, Tokyo, July 13, 1937. *Ibid.*, pp. 319–20.

[88] Memorandum by Mr. Hornbeck, July 13, 1937. 793.94/8737, 8922, MS, Department of State.

[89] Memorandum by Secretary Hull, July 13, 1937. *United States and Japan, 1931–1941*, I, 320–22.

[90] Ambassador Grew to Secretary Hull, Tokyo, July 13, 1937. 793.94/8741, MS, Department of State.

[91] Ambassador Grew to Secretary Hull, Tokyo, July 13, 1937. 793.94/8742, MS, Department of State.

[92] Ambassador Grew to Secretary Hull, Tokyo, July 13, 1937. 793.94/8745, MS, Department of State.

After Secretary Hull had made it clear to the British Foreign Office that he preferred to follow a policy along independent rather than joint lines, he issued (July 16) a public statement indicating the attitude of the Department of State with reference to the situation in the Far East. He began by expressing a viewpoint which had become quite familiar: "There can be no serious hostilities anywhere in the world which will not in one way or another affect interests or rights or obligations of this country." American policy, therefore, strongly accented the importance of settling international disputes by peaceful means. Other items in the American creed were then cited: "We advocate national and international self-restraint. We advocate abstinence by all nations from use of force in pursuit of policy and from interference in the internal affairs of other nations."[93]

It was significant that this statement was in general and not in regional terms. There was no mention of the basic principles that had controlled American policy in the Far East: the Open Door and the maintenance of Chinese territorial integrity. It was evident that Secretary Hull was feeling his way with great care and still hoped for a peaceful settlement of the Peiping Incident. On July 21 he repeated to Ambassador Saito his earnest desire for peace in the Far East and gave further assurances of his "impartial" attitude towards both nations.[94] When Ambassador Grew communicated to the Japanese Foreign Minister these sentiments of Secretary Hull, Hirota replied that he was still hopeful for peace. Everything depended upon the execution of "the agreement drawn up on July 11 and signed on July 19 by General Chang." Japan was not asking Nanking to recognize the agreement "but only that it shall withhold obstruction."[95] . . .

On July 16, Ambassador Grew reported from Tokyo that "the steady development of plans of the Chinese Government to mobilize its forces and to concentrate them in North China was the principal cause for the decision taken yesterday by the Japanese Government to send reinforcements from Japan to North China." In this connection, the Ho-Umedzu Agreement of July 6, 1935, was of prime importance. In accordance with the terms of this instrument Chinese troops would be withdrawn from Hopeh Province. If they were sent into that province during the present difficulty, war pressures might quickly develop.[96] On July 19 the Chinese Foreign Office sent a note to Japan offering an armistice and further diplomatic negotiations designed to find some formula of settlement. This proposal was obviously unsatisfactory to the Japanese Government which adhered to the viewpoint that the Peiping Incident had been settled by the agreement of July 11. The matter was one that concerned only the local authorities. It was essential, therefore, that the agreement of July 11 be carried out without any obstructions from Nanking. The fact that the Chinese military commander in North China had permitted his troops to cross the Ho-Umedzu line was an indication that he was looking for trouble.[97]

There was another factor in this grave

[93] Statement of Secretary Hull, July 16, 1937. *United States and Japan, 1931–1941*, I, 325–26.

[94] Memorandum by Secretary Hull, July 21, 1937. *Ibid.*, pp. 330–32.

[95] Memorandum by Ambassador Grew, July 22, 1937. *Ibid.*, pp. 333–34.

[96] Ambassador Grew to Secretary Hull, Tokyo, July 16, 1937. 793.94/8789, MS, Department of State.

[97] Ambassador Grew to Secretary Hull, Tokyo, July 20, 1937. 793.94/8863, MS, Department of State.

Far Eastern equation. The Communists were evidently pushing for a clash between the Nationalist armies and the Japanese. On July 16 the counselor of the Japanese Embassy in Nanking (Hidaka) complained to the Chinese Foreign Office that "an additional and very important element of danger has been injected into the situation by the Communists (he implied that he meant the Comintern and the Soviet Government) who 'are attempting to aggravate the trouble between China and Japan.' " Hidaka also let it be known that he had been told by "a high Chinese official" that the "Chinese Government had been intercepting telegrams from Moscow to agents in China which revealed these activities."[98]

The Department of State Insists upon an Independent Policy

In London, Anthony Eden felt increasing concern over the developments in the Far East. On July 20 he had a talk with Ambassador Bingham and expressed the view that the "situation" in North China "had taken a grave turn for the worse." He felt "himself barren of ideas, [but] said he would welcome any suggestions from the American Government as to any action which might tend towards appeasement. . . . He understood and fully agreed with the Secretary of State's position that American action and British action should be along parallel lines, and was confident that separate action by the two Governments with the same objective would have . . . greater weight than any action by his Government alone."[99]

On the evening of July 20, Eden suddenly reverted to his former belief in the efficacy of Anglo-American joint action and inquiry was made whether the Department of State would agree to this approach.[100] Secretary Hull promptly replied that he believed "the course of action thus far pursued" by both governments had "been truly co-operative and that . . . [they] should again, each in his own way, urge upon the Japanese and Chinese Governments the importance of maintaining peace."[101]

After the Department of State had carried out this item, word came from China that Chiang Kai-shek had indicated to the British Ambassador at Nanking that he was willing to carry on negotiations with the Japanese Government but this information could best be imparted to Tokyo by some neutral nation with large interests in the Far East. Britain had indicated to Chiang that this task could not be undertaken by any British diplomat.[102] Chiang then told Ambassador Johnson that "the Central Government of China, out of a sincere desire for peace, had acceded to Japanese demands and had withdrawn its opposition to a local settlement of the Marco Polo Bridge Incident . . . along the lines of the three points covered by the settlement of July 11."[103]

This apparently pacific disposition on the part of Chiang Kai-shek was reassuring to many persons interested in Far Eastern development, and they felt even more optimistic when they read in the

---

[98] Mr. Peck to Secretary Hull, Nanking, July 17, 1937. 793.94/8812, MS, Department of State.

[99] Ambassador Bingham to Secretary Hull, London, July 20, 1937. 793.94/8875, MS, Department of State.

[100] Ambassador Bingham to Secretary Hull, London, July 21, 1937. 793.94/8877, MS, Department of State.

[101] Secretary Hull to the American Embassy in London, July 21, 1937. 793.94/8920, MS, Department of State.

[102] Ambassador Johnson to Secretary Hull, Peiping, July 13, 1937. 793.94/8936, MS, Department of State.

[103] Ambassador Johnson to Secretary Hull, Nanking, July 25, 1937. 793.94/8980, MS, Department of State.

Paris *Soir* the following statement by the Japanese Ambassador in Paris: "I do not look for anything grave. To people who ask whether we want to go to war with China, I simply reply: 'We are really not so stupid.' "[104]

But Japan could be pushed into war through Chinese intransigence. On July 27 the situation in North China took a definite turn for the worse. According to Japanese accounts, Chinese troops attacked a Japanese force at Lanfang and then entrapped a "Japanese force at the southwest gate of Peiping."[105] This news led Secretary Hull to cable to the American ambassadors in Peiping and Tokyo and instruct them "to confer immediately with the British Embassies and in their discretion to take action on lines parallel with the British action toward dissuading the Japanese authorities from proceeding with any plan for military operations which would be likely to endanger the lives of American nationals."[106]
. . .

Secretary Hull was interested in the type of proposals that Secretary Eden wished to place before Japan. On July 29 he forwarded this question to Eden who had no ready answer. The French Foreign Office was equally devoid of ideas. When Bullitt paid a visit to the Quai d'Orsay, Delbos declined "to discuss the position in the Far East. He said that in fact China was isolated though he was definitely opposed to an appeal by China to the League of Nations. The League . . . today was a cipher and the only result of a Chinese appeal would be [that]

the cipher would become the shadow of a cipher. . . . He favored . . . an appeal by China to the signatories of the Nine-Power Pact. . . . He was certain that at the present moment the Soviet Union would do nothing to aid China. Indeed, he had just received a telegram from the French Ambassador in Nanking stating that Chiang Kai-shek was furious with the Russians. The Russians had led him to believe that they would support him and now had told him that they would do nothing."[107]

After having induced Chiang Kai-shek to follow a policy that would lead to war with Japan, Russia then promptly betrayed him. On July 30, Ambassador Bullitt talked to the Russian representative in Paris who "expressed the opinion that his government would do nothing whatsoever to assist China at the present time."[108] Chiang then turned to the United States. The Chinese Ambassador in London strongly pushed the matter of an invocation of the Nine-Power Pact, but he soon conceived the idea that the American Government was holding Britain back. When this viewpoint was presented to Mr. Hornbeck, assurances were immediately given that the Department of State had been "constantly in consultation" with the British Foreign Office and was "neglecting nothing" that would help to settle the situation in the Far East.[109] . . .

On August 6, J. L. Dodds, the British

[104] Paris *Soir*, July 26, 1937.

[105] Memorandum of a conversation between Mr. Suma and Mr. Hornbeck, July 27, 1937. 793.94/9309, MS, Department of State.

[106] Secretary Hull to Ambassador Bingham, July 27, 1937. 793.94/8993, MS, Department of State.

[107] Ambassador Bullitt to Secretary Hull, Paris, July 30, 1937. 793.94/9097, MS, Department of State.

[108] Ambassador Bullitt to Secretary Hull, Paris, July 30, 1937. 793.94/9098-99, MS, Department of State.

[109] Memorandum of a conversation between the Chinese Ambassador (C. T. Wang) and Mr. Hornbeck, July 31, 1937. 793.94/9312, MS, Department of State.

chargé d'affaires in Tokyo, and Ambassador Grew had a conference concerning the situation in Japan and came to the conclusion that an offer of mediation should be extended to the Chinese and Japanese governments. The chances of acceptance were "small but not necessarily hopeless."[110] Grew thought that the offer to the Japanese Government should take the form of an "oral, confidential, semi-informal and exploratory conversation with the Minister for Foreign Affairs." The Department of State agreed with this suggestion and authorized him, when the British chargé was ready to take action, to approach the "Japanese Minister for Foreign Affairs along the lines indicated."[111]

While this instruction was en route to Tokyo, Ambassador Bullitt talked with H. H. Kung in Paris about the Far Eastern crisis. In answer to a question concerning the possibility of a large-scale war, Kung replied that "General Chiang personally wished to fight but that there was much opposition to fighting in the most influential circles in Nanking." Kung then soberly added: "I'm afraid he [Chiang] will fight." In discussing China's finances, Kung said that he "considered it of the utmost importance that the $50,000,000 loan with regard to which he had talked with the President, Jesse Jones, and Pierson, should go through. . . . He had talked with Maisky, Soviet Ambassador in London, who had assured him that if the United States, England and France would make a joint protest against Japan's action and would offer mediation, and if Japan should re-

ject the offer, the Soviet Union would go to war on the side of China."[112]

It is evident that Chiang Kai-shek, under the impact of continued Russian promises of armed assistance, "personally wished to fight." There was little chance that any offer of mediation would be accepted. But the Department of State knew little of the real situation in Nanking: peace seemed just around the corner of a friendly conference. On August 10, Grew informed Hirota that he had been instructed to present a "definite offer of good offices" in an "informal, confidential and exploratory way." If a meeting could be arranged between "Japanese and Chinese plenipotentiaries" at some convenient neutral spot, some formula of peace might be worked out. Hirota expressed his appreciation of this offer of mediation but he added that negotiations were in progress between Ambassador Kawagoe and Mr. Kao, of the Chinese Foreign Office. War might "still be avoided if Chiang Kai-shek would respond with some 'proposal' which could serve as a basis for negotiations."[113]

There was little hope that Chiang would make such a proposal. On August 12, Ambassador Johnson reported that he had been

reliably informed that Chu Teh and Mao Tze Tung, military leaders of the Communistic forces in Shensi, visited Nanking within past few days as sequel to an earlier visit by Chou En-lai, Secretary-General of the Communistic regime at Yennan, Shensi, and that an agreement was reached for the cooperation

---

[110] Joseph C. Grew, *Ten Years in Japan* (New York, 1944), pp. 214–16.

[111] Secretary Hull to Ambassador Bingham, August 7, 1937. 793.94/9217, MS, Department of State.

[112] Ambassador Bullitt to Secretary Hull, Paris, August 6, 1937. 793.94/9220, MS, Department of State.

[113] Memorandum by Ambassador Grew, August 10, 1937. *United States and Japan, 1931–1941*, I, 339–41.

of the Communistic forces with Government troops against the Japanese.[114]

The Scene Shifts to Shanghai

While diplomats talked, the armies of Japan moved ahead in Manchuria. By August 1, Tientsin had fallen and Chinese troop concentrations in the Peiping area had been bombed by the active Japanese air force. Soon Japanese troops occupied the entire Hopeh Province, and the American public was shocked by stories of rape and looting. When the scene shifted to Shanghai there were detailed accounts of Japanese brutality that made an indelible impression upon Secretary Hull. The city did not fall to the Japanese until November 9, and during this long period of military activity there were many incidents that disturbed the Department of State.

Before heavy fighting started in the Shanghai area, Sumner Welles submitted to Secretary Hull a memorandum which emphasized the opinion that Japan would "neither be deterred from fighting China by financial considerations nor, if the two countries fight, find herself hamstrung and compelled to forego her objectives in consequence of financial exhaustion."[115]

On the same day, Mr. Hornbeck submitted a memorandum which dealt specifically with Shanghai. He thought the Secretary of State might "reasonably suggest to and even urge upon the Chinese Government that it withdraw troops which it apparently has introduced . . . into the area around Shanghai which falls within the so-called 'demilitarized zone' which was set up by agreement

between the Japanese and the Chinese in 1932. . . . Regardless of reasons or rights, those [Chinese] troops are not needed there for purposes of maintaining order; . . . they serve as an irritant to the Japanese."[116]

When Japanese marines landed in Shanghai on August 11 this question of the "demilitarized zone" immediately arose. But the Chinese mayor of the city stated that he and the local garrison commander had "no control over the Chinese troops of 88th Division arriving in the area." Their commander was "somewhere in the rear."[117] On August 13 large Japanese reinforcements arrived in Shanghai and during the next ten days there was severe fighting with large casualties. The inevitable "incidents" now occurred. On August 14 the Commander in Chief of the United States Asiatic Fleet sent to the American Embassy in Nanking a telegram requesting him to make a "vigorous protest to Chinese Government of bombing American vessel Shanghai by Chinese planes. Two bombs dropped within 20 yards of *Augusta*. . . . In case any further bombing of U. S. vessels will use anti-aircraft battery in self-defence."[118] This telegram was supported by a similar message from Consul General Gauss to Secretary Hull: "Repeated and increasingly heavy bombing by Chinese planes is continuing. Several bombs have dropped within area of foreign refuge near waterfront. . . . Chinese planes are not respecting Settlement or

[114] Ambassador Johnson to Secretary Hull, Nanking, August 12, 1937. 793.94/9297, MS, Department of State.

[115] Memorandum of Sumner Welles for Secretary Hull, August 10, 1937. 793.94/9487, MS, Department of State.

[116] Memorandum of Mr. Hornbeck for Secretary Hull, August 12, 1937. 793.94/9940, MS, Department of State.

[117] Consul General Gauss to Secretary Hull, Shanghai, August 12, 1937. 793.94/9305, MS, Department of State.

[118] Commander in Chief of the United States Asiatic Fleet to the American Embassy in Nanking, August 13, 1937. FW 793.94/9351, MS, Department of State.

area of refuge. I urge strongest representations to the Generalissimo." [119] On August 15 the chairman of the Shanghai Municipal Council sent an urgent message to the "Consul General for Norway and Senior Consul" asking him to convey "to the Chinese Authorities the most solemn protest against the tragic and unpardonable bombing yesterday of part of the International Settlement, which was known to be entirely free of belligerent troops."[120] Three days later, Consul General Gauss informed Secretary Hull that "despite fact that Chinese have been informed officially that American tenders carrying women and children would leave Shanghai at a stated hour on yesterday, Chinese planes appeared over the area precisely at the hour of departure resulting in Japanese anti-aircraft fire until they were driven away."[121]

In order to check this lawlessness and find some path to peace, the British chargé d'affaires (August 18) presented to the Japanese Foreign Office a proposal that if both the Chinese and Japanese governments would agree to withdraw their armed forces from the Shanghai area and would agree that the protection of Japanese nationals in the International Settlement be entrusted to foreign authorities, His Majesty's Government would be "prepared to undertake this responsibility if other Powers will join them in doing so."[122] The Japanese For-

eign Office did not accept this suggestion. When Secretary Hull heard from Ambassador Grew to this effect, he informed the British Foreign Office that there was no use in having the Department of State support the British proposal.[123]

As the clash between Chinese and Japanese forces at Shanghai continued, Chinese planes seemed unable to avoid bombing American ships. Even the Chinese shore batteries were careless in directing their fire. On the evening of August 20 a shell exploded on the deck of the United States cruiser *Augusta*, killing one seaman and wounding eighteen others.[124] Three days later two "air bombs," believed to be of "Chinese origin," were dropped in the International Settlement, seriously injuring an American citizen.[125] But Secretary Hull was far more interested in reports of Japanese bombing of Nanking than in Chinese bombing of the International Settlement in Shanghai. On September 1, Ambassador Grew called at the Foreign Office to present a protest against Japanese bombing operations "in various parts of China." Hirota replied that "it was the intention of the Japanese forces in China to attack only military establishments but that mistakes were unfortunately inevitable." He then reported to Mr. Grew the lawless situation in Tsingtao since the removal of Japanese nationals. He thought it might be expedient for the powers to "make representations in Nanking" with regard to this situation. Turning to the matter of Sino-

---

119 Consul General Gauss to Secretary Hull, Shanghai, August 14, 1937. 793.94/9348, MS, Department of State.

120 C. S. Franklin, chairman of the Shanghai Municipal Council, to the consul general for Norway, August 15, 1937. 793.94/10595, MS, Department of State.

121 Consul General Gauss to Secretary Hull, Shanghai, August 18, 1937. 793.94/9467, MS, Department of State.

122 Ambassador Grew to Secretary Hull, Tokyo, August 18, 1937. 793.94/9470, MS, Department of State.

123 Secretary Hull to Ambassador Grew, August 19, 1937. 793.94/9470, MS, Department of State.

124 Consul General Gauss to Secretary Hull, Shanghai, August 21, 1937. 793.94/9565, MS, Department of State.

125 Ambassador Johnson to Secretary Hull, Nanking, August 27, 1937. 793.94/9746, MS, Department of State.

Soviet relations he remarked that the recent conclusion of a pact between China and Russia might have unfortunate results. There was "grave danger of the communists getting control in China." The communist menace was "very real" because their actual aim was "to take over eventual complete control of the Government and country." With reference to peace in the Far East, the Chinese could have it on three conditions: (1) good relations with Manchuria; (2) withdrawal of Chinese troops from North China; (3) the cessation in China of anti-Japanese activities and propaganda.[126]

The communist menace in China gave Secretary Hull little concern. He was now thoroughly aroused over reports of indiscriminate bombings in China by the Japanese. In a long instruction to Ambassador Grew he spoke his mind very plainly. It appeared to him that Japanese unresponsiveness to American protests against bombings showed that the Japanese Government did not set a high value upon American efforts "to cultivate good will, confidence, and stability in general." If the Japanese Government would just follow the high principles enunciated by the American Government on July 16 the situation in the Far East would probably improve. While the American Government had endeavored to follow an "absolutely impartial course" during the current crisis in China, the actions of the Japanese armed forces had shocked American opinion. It would be expedient for the Japanese Government to keep in mind that their course in China was looked upon in America with the same degree of disapproval that it had evoked in Britain. American public

opinion "has been outraged by the methods and strategy employed by the combatants, particularly by the Japanese military, and has become gradually more critical of Japan." It was high time the Japanese Government gave heed to the principles so often expressed by the Department of State.[127]

It is evident that the statement of American principles by Secretary Hull on July 16 was a verbal bombshell directed against Japan. All talk of an "absolutely impartial course" towards China and Japan during the July crisis was mere diplomatic eyewash which no realistic statesmen took seriously. Hull was definitely antagonistic towards Japan, and his statement of July 16 was a prelude to the quarantine speech of President Roosevelt on October 5. . . .

The quarantine speech of October 5 had many macabre overtones designed to frighten the American people. It indicated that large portions of the world were experiencing a "reign of terror," and that the "landmarks and traditions which have marked the progress of civilization toward a condition of law, order and justice" were being "wiped away." "Innocent peoples and nations" were being "cruelly sacrificed to a greed for power and supremacy" which was "devoid of all sense of justice and humane consideration." If this sad condition of affairs existed in other parts of the world it was vain for anyone to "imagine that America will escape, that it may expect mercy, that this Western Hemisphere will not be attacked, and that it will continue tranquilly and peacefully to carry on the ethics and the arts of civilization."

Newspapers of a one-world persuasion sprang to the President's support. The

[126] Ambassador Grew to Secretary Hull, Tokyo, September 1, 1937. 793.94/9835; memorandum of Ambassador Grew, September 1, 1937. 793.94/10157, MSS, Department of State.

[127] Secretary Hull to Ambassador Grew, September 2, 1937. *United States and Japan, 1931–1941*, I, 361–64.

New York Times and the *World-Tele-gram* promptly attacked the "unrealities of isolation,"[128] while the *New York Daily News* suggested a long-range Anglo-American naval blockade of Japan if that nation were to overrun China and threaten the interests of the Western powers."[129]

Some papers advocated an economic boycott as a means to bring Japan to reason. The *Washington Post* urged that America "immediately cease to buy Japanese goods,"[130] and this opinion was strongly seconded by the *Washington Evening Star*[131] and the Rochester *Democrat and Chronicle*.[132] The *Atlanta Constitution* expressed the emphatic opinion that "war-diseased nations must be quarantined,"[133] and the *Birmingham News*[134] and the Raleigh *News and Observer*[135] joined this chorus. In the Middle West the *Chicago Daily News*,[136] the *St. Louis Globe-Democrat*,[137] and the *Cincinnati Enquirer*[138] expressed agreement with the "general principles" of the President's address. On the Pacific Coast the *San Francisco Chronicle*,[139] the *Los Angeles Times*,[140] and the *Portland Morning Oregonian*[141] adopted a favorable attitude.

But there was a large legion of newspapers that rejected any thought of economic sanctions against Japan. Such

action would lead to war. The *New York Herald Tribune* believed that the President's speech had been based upon the "identical sands of confusion, emotion and wishful thinking which so tragically engulfed Mr. Wilson's great vision."[142] The New York *Sun* warned the President that American public opinion would not approve any policy of "pulling chestnuts out of the fire for any association of foreign nations."[143] The *Boston Herald* boldly declared that "Americans must not embark on another costly attempt to reform the world,"[144] while even the stanchly Democratic *Boston Post* cried out in protest: "He [the President] must know that the American people are in no mood for a crusade."[145]

The *Chicago Tribune* was openly hostile to any threat of a boycott against Japan. Economic sanctions would lead America down the road to war.[146] The *Detroit Free Press* voiced the opinion that there was no "adequate reason for remarks that were evangelistic rather than statesmanlike, and were manifestly designed to stir emotions rather than provoke careful thought."[147] The *Milwaukee Journal* remarked that a boycott is a "first cousin to outright war,"[148] and the Spokane *Spokesman-Review* stated ominously that the President's Chicago address "approximated a declaration of war."[149]

The columnists were divided in their opinions of the Chicago address. Boake Carter was fearful that the President suffered from the "disease of moral fervor

128 October 6, 8, 1937.
129 October 3, 7, 1937.
130 October 8, 1937.
131 October 6, 7, 1937.
132 October 6, 1937.
133 October 7, 1937.
134 October 6, 11, 1937.
135 October 6, 8, 1937.
136 October 6, 8, 1937.
137 October 15, 1937.
138 October 7, 8, 1937.
139 October 6, 1937.
140 October 6, 7, 1937.
141 October 6, 1937.

142 October 6, 8, 1937.
143 October 6, 7, 1937.
144 October 6, 7, 1937.
145 October 11, 1937.
146 October 6, 1937.
147 October 7, 1937.
148 October 10, 1937.
149 October 6, 7, 1937.

for reform."[150] Paul Mallon regarded the address as a clever move to divert attention from the unfortunate appointment of Hugo Black to the Supreme Court,[151] while General Hugh S. Johnson was worried that America, as in 1917, would play the role of "sucker."[152]

On the other hand, David Lawrence hailed the address as the "speech the whole world has been waiting for several months to hear,"[153] Dorothy Thompson was delighted that she could now envisage the end of American "neutrality,"[154] and Walter Lippman praised the President for a much-needed clarion call to the democracies to resist aggressor nations.[155]

The Catholic press had few words of praise for the President's Chicago challenge. *America* flatly stated that the "people of the United States positively are opposed to foreign imbroglios";[156] the *Ave Maria* was filled with misgivings,[157] while Father Gillis, in the *Catholic World*, was sharply critical of any pressure in favor of American intervention in the Far East.[158]

It is interesting to note that the *Christian Century*, which reflected the Protestant viewpoint, was distinctly suspicious of the Chicago speech. In a forecast of the future it warned that if America went to war on behalf of China the result would be a victory for Russia.[159]

This Russian angle of the situation in the Far East was clearly perceived by many observers. On October 12 the Division of Far Eastern Affairs prepared a memorandum for the use of Secretary Hull. With reference to possible economic sanctions, the memorandum asks the question whether the United States should take the lead in such a movement. In answer to this question it remarks: "It is believed that the assuming of such a position by any country would bring that country face to face with a very real hazard. . . . It seems to me [Mr. Hamilton, chief of the Division] that public opinion in the United States is definitely opposed to the United States assuming a position of leadership in the imposing of restrictive measures directed at Japan. Moreover it should be borne in mind that if restrictive measures should take the form of economic 'sanctions,' the United States would be called upon to carry the heaviest burden.[160] . . . If some program could be worked out which would give Japan a reasonable prospect of economic security and which would remove Japan's fear of Communism and attack from the Soviet Union, there would be removed some basic elements in the situation responsible for Japan's present imperialistic program."[161]

---

[150] *Boston Daily Globe,* October 8, 1937.

[151] *Boston Herald,* October 8, 1937.

[152] *New York World-Telegram,* October 6, 1937.

[153] *Chicago Daily News,* October 7, 1937.

[154] *New York Herald Tribune,* October 10, 1937.

[155] *New York Herald Tribune* October 16, 1937.

[156] October 16, 1937.

[157] October 23, 1937, pp. 534–35.

[158] December 1937, pp. 257–65. On October 9, 1937, Senator David I. Walsh wrote a note to Secretary Hull in which he inclosed a telegram from the Maryknoll Fathers in Japan. They deeply regretted the "recent change official attitude towards Sino-Japanese trouble," and urgently requested his influence "towards restoring previous attitude impartial tolerance as most practical policy." 793.94/10546, MS, Department of State.

[159] October 20, 1937, pp. 1287–88.

[160] In a letter to Mr. Hornbeck, Mr. Taneo Taketa, a representative of the South Manchuria Railway, points out the close economic ties between the United States and Japan. The South Manchuria Railway alone had purchased "far more than $100,000,000 worth of equipment from the United States." Other firms had purchased large amounts. 793.94/10708, MS, Department of State.

[161] Memorandum prepared by the Division of Far Eastern Affairs, October 12, 1937. 793.94/10706, MS, Department of State.

Herbert Feis: THE ROAD TO PEARL HARBOR

After Our Elections: Steps towards a Concerted Program

NOVEMBER 1940; the Roosevelt administration was safely confirmed in power. It could properly construe the election result as approval of its opposition to the Axis and its support of Britain short of war. But, because of the terms in which he had expounded these policies during the campaign, the President was obliged still to move warily and on the slant. The words spoken during the election contest lived on to complicate and confine decision for the times ahead.

Americans had been told that they need not take part in the battles then being fought in Europe and Asia and that the government would not cause them to do so.[1] They had been urged to provide weapons and resources to fend off the danger of having to go to war. British resistance, the expressed thought ran, was giving us time to become so strong that no country, or group of countries, would dare attack us. While if the Axis won, the United States would become exposed to its fury and forced to fight near or within our own land. This was a correct judgment of the meaning to us of the wars in Europe and Asia. It was a well founded basis for the program sponsored by the government and for the acceptance of the connected risks. But it left the President open to a charge of blunder or bad faith if the United States found itself at war.

The government avoided all actions which could not be construed as defensive. It continued — and it was no easy thing to do — to refuse to enter into any accord which carried an obligation to go to war. But it shaped our policies in conference with other governments and fitted its action to theirs. We were about to form a common front against Japan without admitting it or promising to maintain it by force.

Before leaving the subject, a comment may be added about the information given the American people during the months after the election— the winter of 1940–41. Some things that were done were wholly told, some vaguely told,

---

[1] The most unguarded of these statements, amounting to a promise, was made by the President in a speech in Boston on October 30 when he said:

"And while I am talking to you mothers and fathers, I give you one more assurance.

"I have said this before, but I shall say it again and again and again:

"Your boys are not going to be sent into any foreign wars.

"They are going into training to form a force so strong that, by its very existence, it will keep the threat of war far away from our shores.

"The purpose of our defense is defense."

It can, of course, be well argued that the question of what is or is not a "foreign war" is not to be learned from a map alone. But the manner in which it was used during the campaign seemed to give it a simple meaning of wars fought in and by foreign countries. The term was, unless I am mistaken, taken over from the opponents of intervention. A cousinly term was effectively used by Charles A. Beard in the title of a virulent article that be published in *Harper's Magazine* for September 1939, "Giddy Minds and Foreign Quarrels."

Willkie spoke in the same strain as Roosevelt; in fact he set the pace in providing assurance that the United States need not and should not enter the war. The isolationists were far more extreme, denouncing any and all acts of intervention.

From *The Road to Pearl Harbor* by Herbert Feis (Princeton: Princeton University Press, 1950), excerpted material from pages 133–328. Reprinted by permission.

and a few, such as naval talks and movements, were hardly told at all. The President's utterances of this period did not provide all the explanatory knowledge that could have been wanted to follow and judge American policy in action. For they were not systematic statements of the situation facing the United States and the choice before it. They were emotional appeals to the American people to hurry along their military preparations and to stand firm and hard against the Axis. They were written as such, not by essayists but by political advisers and dramatists. They were pin-pointed explosives.[2] They were exertions of leadership in behalf of measures that were secretly in the making, or rather in the taking. . . .

The whole range of methods of restraining Japan was, during November and December, again inspected in Washington. There were three main ways in which we might try to do so. Japan might be deprived of the means of sustaining a long war; ships and planes might be moved into the threatened regions; China might be so assisted as to be a continued worry and drain. Each of these measures had its advocates; each was in some measure deemed feasible. But each could turn out to be a blunder that would take the United States into war, and maybe a losing one. The assignment was to use each in the right degree and at the right time.

Of the three, the further control of exports of Japan seemed the best justified. As already noted, the remaining trade was almost wholly a brokerage in

war materials.[3] Prospectively we or Britain might need everything that was being sent.

On November 1 Lothian reported his government to be most seriously disturbed at this contribution to Japan's war power. It asked the American government to join the British Dominions and Empire in limiting the total export to Japan of all essential goods to what could be deemed "normal" amounts. There was a suspicion that some of the excess was going to Germany over the Trans-Siberian Railway. A few days later the State Department was notified that a proposal to this end had been put before the Dominions, India, and Burma, and was being discussed with the Dutch government. And a few days after that it was urged that oil shipments be similarly restricted if, as the British thought, Japanese war stocks were greater than the American government had reckoned.[4] This last suggestion was sent on to Admiral Stark with the request that if the Navy felt inclined to send an answer, it should please get in touch with the State Department before doing so.

The American agencies responsible

[2] To adopt a description used by Robert E. Sherwood — *Roosevelt and Hopkins* (New York, 1948), p. 184 — who writes that Willkie's radio speeches "sounded" harsh, hurried and diffuse — short-range blasts of birdshot rather than pin-pointed high explosive shells."

[3] As described by the President of the Planning Board to the Privy Council on September 26: "In our mobilization plan on materials the center of gravity is laid on the items for military purposes." Washington did not have to hear these words to know the fact; the trade statistics told the story.

[4] A British memorandum (of November 20) on this subject alluded to a supposed estimate of the American Navy, placing Japan's stocks as approximately 37 million barrels. This reference was a puzzle since the naval estimates known to the State and Treasury Departments were much higher, about 70 million barrels (Morgenthau diary, October 2, 1940). Perhaps there were several naval estimates in circulation; perhaps the figure cited in the estimate to which the British Embassy alluded referred only to stocks held by the Japanese Navy, and was misunderstood by it.

for the production of weapons greatly
wanted to act along this line. Stimson
and Morgenthau also, as before, favored
it. Knox seemed more than ready to go
along, although Stark and other of the
highest officers in the Navy still seemed
of two minds. It was the State Department, almost alone, which continued to
hold off action.

The long and tired meetings within
Hull's office ended in a different assessment of risks. On the one hand, American reports did not validate the sharp
British fear that Japan was about to attack Singapore or the Indies. On the
other hand, they warned anew that economic action would not avert war in the
Far East; but, on the contrary (as Grew
wrote to the President on December 14),
"would tend to push the Japanese people
onward in a forlorn hope of making
themselves economically self-sufficient."[5]

This being so, Hull insisted that it was
wise not to provoke Japan further until
and unless American and British forces
in the Far East were stronger. He would

not, he retorted to critics, give assent to
any step that might mean war in the
Pacific until he knew the Navy was
ready, until he knew that our ships were
where they would be needed and prepared to fight. The Navy, or rather its
senior admirals, were saying that they
were not. And when Hull set about
trying to get part of the fleet dispatched
to the Far East — as he did — the Navy
resisted.

The British government was eager to
see our ships move. On November 23
word was sent of an intended reinforce-
ment of Malaya by Australian and New
Zealand soldiers. Would not, the query
was transmitted from London, the American fleet in the Pacific use Singapore as
a base, or at least send some ships there?
This was a proposal for the division of
the Pacific fleet.[6] Time and again during
the coming months it was to be repeated
with unrepressed anxiety. As it was by
Lothian, who, just back from consultation with Churchill and the cabinet, told
Hull two days later (on November 25)
that his government definitely expected
Japan to attack Singapore. And as it
was again by the Australian Minister on
December 3.[7]

These pleas came from knowledge that
in the event that Japan did strike, Britain would not be able to protect the
threatened colonies. All its ships and
planes were needed in the Atlantic and
Mediterranean, and even there were los-

---

[5] Grew's many messages during November and
December contained repeated statements of this
conclusion, partly out of fear that the opposite
one might have drawn from his "green light"
telegram of September 12. On November 3, for
example, he cabled: "the view that war in the
Far East can thus be averted by continuation of
trade embargoes and, as proposed by some, the
imposition of a blockade is not supported by
what has thus far occurred."

But while his warnings were clear, his advice
as to what policy the United States should follow was not clear. In some messages he seemed
to approve further pressure on Japan despite the
risk. Thus, for example, November 7 he cabled:
"I believe that while the continuance of a firm
policy by the United States would involve inevitable risks, nevertheless, a policy of laissez-
faire would lead to dangers of greater magni-
tude." Nor does the explanation he gave to the
Pearl Harbor Committee (*Pearl Harbor Attack*,
Part 2, p. 617, *et seq.*) seem to me to make the
intended purport of his advice during this period
any clearer.

[6] As expounded by the First Sea Lord, Sir Dudley
Pound, to the American naval mission in London,
it was essential to hold Singapore at all costs.
With the American fleet, or a substantial part of
it, based on Singapore, Japan, he argued, would
be much less likely to risk war and if war came
the Japanese fleet could be contained north of
the long chain of islands comprising the Dutch
East Indies.

[7] Hull's memo of this talk with Lothian is printed,
ibid., Part 20, pp. 4072–74.

ing out. Unless the United States acted as shield, there was no shield.

Hull and Admiral Stark, to whom the British proposals were primarily directed, let them rest. The British government accepted the decision. But the same proposals about sending the American fleet to Singapore were waiting for Harry Hopkins in London when he arrived in January. This avoidance caused a temporary sag in the chain of resolution to confine Japan. The British would not give the Indies a promise to come to its defense. This caused the Indies government to state that it would oppose any further steps that would arouse Japan.[8] The Australian government also began to cool towards the proposals for joint economic action.[9]

The American government would not have the American fleet display itself in the threatened zones. It would not promise to join in their defense if they were attacked. But it was willing to plan in conference how the forces of all the opponents of Japan could best be used in concert or combination, if the United States should find itself fighting by the side of others. Staff talks for that purpose between the British and Dutch in Singapore and Batavia — with an officer of the American Navy in attendance — had thus far come to little.

On November 12 Stark recommended to the President that Army and Navy

representatives be authorized to enter at once "upon an exhaustive series of secret staff conversations with the British, from which definite plans and agreements to promote unity of effort against the Axis and Japan could emerge."[10] Marshall concurred and the President approved. When on the 25th the British government said that "at once" was none too soon, Hull agreed. Upon doing so, he observed that "of course there could be no agreement entered into in this respect, but that there should undoubtedly be a collaboration with the view of making known to each other any and all information practicable in regard to what both might have in mind to do, and when and where, in case of a military move by Japan in the south or some other direction."

The invitation was sent off (November 30) in the form of a personal bid from Stark to the British Chiefs of Staff to send accredited representatives — before Christmas, if possible. They would, it was understood, work out further with our staff how all the opposed forces could

---

[8] The Governor-General of the Indies sent word to this effect on Dec. 5 through the Dutch Ambassador in Washington, Loudon; he said he would not agree to the dispatch of American naval observers to the Indies or talk about possible naval bases.

[9] The Australian Minister for Foreign Affairs on December 10 pointed out that his country could not use economic sanctions with the same impunity as the United States. At the same time he brought up the possibility of an American naval visit to Australia.

[10] Samuel Eliot Morison, *History of the United States Naval Operations in World War II; The Battle of the Atlantic* (Boston, 1947), I, 43–44.

This memorandum of Stark's was a lucid statement of the problems and burdens of an unlimited war with Japan and a convincing presentation of the opinion that the primary way to protect principal American interests was to assure the continued existence of the British Empire. Accordingly it recommended that even if forced into war with Japan, the United States should plan to avoid operations in the Far East and Middle Pacific that would prevent the Navy from moving to the Atlantic forces adequate to safeguard our interests and policies in the event of a British collapse. This argument was adopted as basic American strategy and remained so.

As revised by the Joint Planning Committee of the Army and Navy it became at once the basis of the preparatory talks between our Special Naval Observer in London (Admiral Ghormley) and the British Admiralty in preparation for the Combined Staff meetings that opened in Washington in January 1941.

be best used to sustain the battle against Germany, and prevent or defeat an attack by Japan. The military men were to be allowed to erect models for possible action. But they were forbidden to say whether their governments would use or follow the models. It was not going to prove easy for them, as the talks went on, to heed this injunction.[11] For it became more and more unreal in the face of what their governments were doing — by mutual accord — both in the Atlantic and Pacific.

While keeping the American fleet at American bases, while refusing to say what it would or would not do if Japan sailed into the Southwest Pacific, the American government — within a month after the elections — put together a program of subtly adjusted measures to hinder Japan.

First came the decisions in regard to aid for China in response to Chiang Kai-shek's appeals. On November 30 the President announced that we would put another 100 million dollars at his disposal. Fifty modern pursuit planes at once were promised him, with as many more as possible. Steps were taken to issue passports to American citizens who wished to go to China to serve as aviators or aviation in-

structors. A plan for providing China with long-range bombers so that it could hit back at Tokyo was excitedly discussed with the British and Chinese. To the chagrin of all, it was found impractical.[12] These measures were the outcome of a tense effort to make sure that the Chiang Kai-shek regime would be able and willing to keep in the fight.

Ships and planes were sent out to the Philippines. Six submarines went, with more to follow. Plans were made to assemble the whole Asiatic fleet at Manila and to increase its size. Hull urged that the Navy send as well a whole squadron of cruisers to southernmost Philippine ports. The President was briefly for this, but changed his mind. He also wanted to publish the news of our naval movements, but he took Hull's advice to let them become known by reports that were certain to seep out, as the ships were seen. A public announcement, he thought, might cause trouble of two kinds: objection within the United States which would lessen the effect upon Japan; and excitement within Japan. Japan was not to be threatened publicly, but to be left guessing.

[11] The difficulty of avoiding misunderstanding was foreseen. Thus Admiral Hart, Commander in Chief of the Asiatic Fleet, wrote to Admiral Stark on November 18: "It should be possible, without making any political commitment, or without prejudging our final decision in each case to proceed on certain assumptions. For instance, that in the event of a Jap attack on the Netherlands East Indies we will intervene if the British do, and then carry on with the British (and the Dutch, if they are willing) the extensive conversations which that assumption necessitates. It is realized, however, that in practice there lies danger of certain implications of actually having made political commitments by the very fact of accepting such an assumption as having elements of possibility."

[12] This seems to have been inspired by a remark of the President that it would be a good thing if the Chinese could bomb Japan. Morgenthau took it up, and talked it over with Lothian and T. V. Soong who enthusiastically cabled Chiang Kai-shek. Hull said he was for it, but it might occur to skeptical spirits who knew him that he saw no need to catch that arrow in his hand since it would soon fall to earth. Chiang Kai-shek answered that he would carry out the plan, provided the United States supplied not only the bombers but escort planes and the necessary ground organization. We, of course, had none of these to spare; the bombers would have had to be taken from the allotments destined for Britain, Hawaii, and the Philippines. The idea was dropped at a meeting on December 23, when General Marshall demonstrated how impractical it was. Morgenthau diary, entries for December 3, 7, 8, 10, 18, 20, 22, and 23, 1940.

"I believed in letting them guess as to when and in what set of circumstances we would fight. While Japan continued to guess, we continued to get ready for anything she might do."[13]

The Japanese were not the only ones compelled to guess. The British were just as uncertain. A month later Harry Hopkins from London was reporting to the President that "Eden asked me repeatedly what our country would do if Japan attacked Singapore or the Dutch East Indies, saying it was essential to their policy to know."[14]

The thought may be carried further. Not only did the British not know what we would do, but neither did Roosevelt or Hull know. Would the President ask Congress to declare war on Japan? Or would he merely take some lesser measures — such as turning submarines over to the British, or using American naval forces to maintain a patrol and convoy system in the Pacific? Or, because that might waste naval forces, would he not even do that?

He was spared the need of deciding. Most fortunately so. For grave uses for the fleet in the Atlantic loomed up more clearly than before, and a great need to face Hitler with unengaged forces. On December 8, Churchill, by letter, put before the President (through Hull) a lucid and compelling summary of the situation faced by Britain and of the aid it would need to carry on. Among its parts were these: "The danger of Great Britain being destroyed by a swift, overwhelming blow has for the time being very greatly receded. In its place there is a long, gradually maturing danger, less sudden and less spectacular, but equally deadly. This mortal danger is the steady and increasing diminution of sea tonnage. . . . The

decision for 1941 lies upon the seas. Unless we can establish our ability to feed this island, to import the munitions of all kinds which we need, unless we can move our armies to the various theatres where Hitler and his confederate Mussolini must be met, and maintain them there . . . we may fall by the way, and the time needed by the United States to complete her defensive preparations may not be forthcoming. It is, therefore, in shipping and in the power to transport across the oceans, particularly the Atlantic Ocean, that in 1941 the crunch of the whole war will be found."[15]

In drafting this, Churchill had before him Stark's memo of November 12. A copy had been sent on to him by the British naval representative in Washington, along with Stark's remark that it would be useful if the Prime Minister endorsed the basic suggestions therein contained. The advice was taken to heart. The Prime Minister's analysis left no doubt that the United States would have to do more than it had done.

While the President was still in the Caribbean, the problem drew together Hull, Knox, Stimson, Stark, and Marshall. They hunted for the response that would be sufficient yet possible. All agreed with the comment that Stimson wrote in his diary while these talks were on: "It is very apparent that nothing will save Great Britain from the starvation of her supplies, which Stark estimates will necessarily take place in six months, except assistance from us by convoy in the Atlantic . . ."[16] When Stimson so proposed in the cabinet (on December 19), "The President said he hadn't quite reached that yet."[17]

13 Hull, *op. cit.*, I, 915.
14 Sherwood, *op. cit.*, p. 259.

15 Winston S. Churchill, *Their Finest Hour* (Boston, 1949), p. 560.
16 Stimson diary, entry for December 16, 1940.
17 *Ibid.*, entry for December 19, 1940.

But, short of that, the resolve emerged from these December conferences to extend American naval protection over the Atlantic as far and as fast as might be necessary, and in the face of any risks of fighting at sea. This was enough (though not the sole) reason for refusing to promise to join the defense of Singapore and the Indies; enough reason why the President could not know or tell what he might do if Japan attacked them. A season was ahead in which the forces of the Allies were to be most wanly stretched. . . .

In the disturbed realm of diplomacy which the United States and Japan had entered, the language used is in part symbolic, in part spoken. Battleships and economic controls are the symbol of power in reserve, symbols used to give edge to verbal warnings, a way of saying "Do you see what I mean?" without saying it. But at the same time the American government was giving secret spoken warnings to Japan.

Dooman, the experienced Counselor of the American Embassy in Tokyo, had been on leave in the United States. He was known by the Japanese to be a firm and straightforward friend. So it was thought that his report of the state of American opinion might be accepted as advice rather than as a threat. On February 14 (Tokyo time) he put before Ohashi, the Vice-Minister for Foreign Affairs, the "philosophy" of the American position. The Vice-Minister was told that the American people were determined to support Britain even at the risk of war; that if Japan or any other country menaced that effort it "would have to expect to come into conflict with the United States"; that if Japan were to occupy Dutch or British areas in the Pacific it would create havoc with the British situation in the war; and that the United States had abstained from an oil embargo

in order not to impel Japan to create a situation that could only lead to the most serious outcome.

On the same date, February 14 (Washington time), the President had his first talk with the new Japanese Ambassador, Admiral Nomura. He made no such blunt affirmations. By being affable and eager, the President sought to show that he wished peace, not war. He spoke as though the danger of war lay in a chance error or incident rather than because of any basic clash of interest. The purpose was to encourage the Japanese government to talk with us. If, as was thought, and correctly thought, in Washington, there was still a division of opinion in the Japanese government, an engagement to talk with us would help the proponents of peace. The light touch was chosen for heavy work, for critical work.[18]

In summary, then, American policy during this winter period of alarm (January-February) was a compound of warning gestures, slowly spreading coercion, earnest advice, and an invitation to talk.

The reports that came back from Tokyo were taken to mean that this policy was, at least for the time being, effective. Grew reported on the 18th of February that the Japanese officials were much disturbed by the reactions abroad; and that Matsuoka was being compelled again to defend himself against criticisms of the Tripartite Pact. The Japanese Foreign Office denied in a calm note on the 20th to the British that there was any basis for their alarm; nor for the warlike preparations which the British and the Americans were taking to meet unreal contingencies in the South Seas.

On February 20, or thereabouts, it became confirmed that Matsuoka was about to leave for Moscow, Berlin, and Rome.

[18] Hull's memorandum of this talk is printed in *Foreign Relations: Japan*, II, 387–89.

"For the purpose," Churchill informed the President, "of covering the failure of action against us."[19] This was not an adequate explanation. But about the direction of Matsuoka's mind at any given moment any guess seemed to be as good as another — so like a twisted rope was he. As when told by Grew that everything that Dooman had said to Ohashi had his (Grew's) entire concurrence and approval, he answered that he entirely agreed with what Dooman had said.[20] To Craigie at about the same time he said that Japan's motto was "No conquest, no oppression, no exploitation."

Matsuoka's words were not trusted. But the allowance of time was a great relief. And beyond that a great chance — both to strive further to avert war with Japan, and to get ready for the fight if war came. Projects for each purpose were in secret course. Two ladders were being built for history; no one knew which would be used. . . .

The proposed agreement turned out to be of great scope and many parts — the meaning of some of which was far from clear. But its main points can be briefly summarized. The Japanese government would have, according to its terms, given two pledges of importance; first, to use only peaceful measures in the Southwest Pacific, and, second, to come to the support of Germany only if that country were the object of an aggressive attack. In return for these promises, the American government was to do several things, among them: to restore normal trade with Japan in so far as the wanted products were available; to assist Japan to obtain the raw materials it wanted from the Southwest Pacific area (that meant oil, rubber, tin, and bauxite); and to ask Chiang Kai-shek to make peace with Japan on terms specified; his regime was to coalesce with the rival created by Japan; if Chiang rejected the request the United States was to end its support of China. Among the other items was a suggestion that the American government give friendly diplomatic assistance "for the removal of Hongkong and Singapore as doorways to further political encroachment by the British in the Far East."

Talk was to roam for many months over each and every one of these matters. The items were reported so often that at times the negotiators became unsure of the connections between them. Nomura once or twice seemed to lose track of which were in and which were out. The phrases were varied as often as a rich dowager changes costume, and the object was usually the same — to enhance the impression without changing the article.

As the skeptical students in the State Department assayed this April text, they found it poor —too poor to use as payment for protection against a Japanese move south. The United States would have been obliged, not only to end aid to China, but to coerce it into accepting permanent Japanese influence in its affairs. It would have been pledged to provide Japan with the means of maintaining whatever size army and navy it wanted. And even then, if Japan should have decided to join in the war against Britain, it would have been free to do so; the Axis connection was not severed.

[19] In this message of February 20, reprinted in *Pearl Harbor Attack*, Part 19, p. 3454, Churchill attributed the postponement of the attack to fear of the United States. He was doing his best to keep the fear alive, as when on the 24th he remarked to the Japanese Ambassador in London that it would be a pity if Japan, already at war with China, should find itself at war with Great Britain and the United States. But he took occasion also to assure the Japanese government that the measures taken by Britain were only for defense, that no attack would be made upon Japan or Japanese forces.

[20] *Foreign Relations: Japan*, II, 143.

Yet no purpose, Hull thought, would be served by an unqualified rejection of this child of chance. It was wise to keep the opinion alive within the Japanese government that the issues dividing the two nations might be settled by talk. It was essential to ward off the conclusion that no path except that of war could take Japan towards its ends. Who knew what turn of battle or new estimate of chances might change the outlook? Thus Hull decided to deal with the proposals gently, to show himself ready to discuss them, and to try to modify them.

Then when he saw Nomura on April 14 he said merely that he would like to know whether the Japanese government wished to present the document which had found its way into the State Department as a first step in negotiations — it being understood both governments could propose changes. Nomura said he was so disposed.[21] Two days later, the news of the Japanese-Soviet neutrality pact having just arrived, the Secretary made a detour of the sort for which he had special talent. Ushering the action in by one octopuslike sentence which it would take a whole chapter of print to dissect, he gave the Ambassador a piece of paper.[22] On it four points were jotted down, about which he invited the comment of the Japanese government as a "paramount preliminary" to the start of the discussions.

In weighing all that came after, these four points should be borne in mind. For they marked out the ground on which the American government stood. In some phases of the talks with Japan, it was deemed discreet to leave them in the background. But they were never forgotten. In order they were:

1. Respect for the territorial integrity and the sovereignty of each and all nations.

2. Support of the principle of non-interference in the internal affairs of other countries.

3. Support of the principle of equality, including equality of commercial opportunity.

4. Non-disturbance of the *status quo* in the Pacific except as the *status quo* may be altered by peaceful means.

The Japanese government did not want to argue principles; abstract principles, which took no account of place, time, or degree. It wanted an end to American aid to China, a lifting of the embargoes, economic independence, a commanding place in the Far East. Thus, the Japanese records verify, it studied this list of commandments glumly. They made a cavern in which Japan could become lost and delayed. But the Japanese government was to find that there was no way round them. Or, as the matter was regarded by the heads of that government (and so stated in their later defense), American insistence that Japan subscribe to these four principles was "symptomatic of a doctrinairism which was to exercise a baleful influence throughout.". . .[23]

On July 2 there came together in the presence of the Emperor the chief figures of the civil and military governments of Japan. These included the Prime Minister, Prince Konoye; the Foreign Minister, Matsuoka; the Minister for War, General Tojo; the Minister for the Navy, Admiral Oikawa; the Chief of the Army General Staff, General Sugiyama; the Chief of the Naval General Staff, Admiral Nagano; the President of the Privy Council, Hara; and the Minister for Home Affairs, Hiranuma. The plans ratified at this Imperial Conference set into determined motion the

---

[21] Hull's memorandum of this talk is printed, *ibid.*, II, 402, *et seq.*

[22] *Ibid.*, II, 406–7.

[23] *Far East Mil. Trib.*, Defense Document No. 3100.

acts and responses that six months later resulted in war between Japan and the United States. The tail of the serpent wound round to its mouth.

From the text of the resolution adopted at this conference the course of events that followed can now be clearly traced. It is not very long and the reader, I think, will want to have most of it:[24]

An Outline of the Policy of the Imperial Government in View of Present Developments
(Decision reached at the Conference held in the Imperial Presence on July 2)

I. Policy
1. The Imperial Government is determined to follow a policy which will result in the establishment of the Greater East Asia Co-Prosperity Sphere and world peace, no matter what international developments take place.

2. The Imperial Government will continue its effort to effect a settlement of the China Incident and seek to establish a solid basis for the security and preservation of the nation. This will involve an advance into the southern regions and, depending on future developments, a settlement of the Soviet Question as well.

3. The Imperial Government will carry out the above program no matter what obstacles may be encountered.

[24] I have selected the translation of this "Outline of the Policy of the Imperial Government in View of Present Developments" contained in the "Konoye Memoirs" (as printed in *Pearl Harbor Attack*, Part 20, pp. 4018–19), in preference to that contained in the text presented to the *International Military Tribunal* (Exh. No. 588). Between these two translations there are points of difference, both in the order of exposition and in the tone, though no basic difference in meaning. The translation presented to the *International Military Tribunal* reads as though the Japanese government were virtually determined on war with the United States, while the one herein used seems to regard that event as a possibility against which Japan was to prepare but still seek to avoid.

II. Summary
1. Steps will be taken to bring pressure on the Chiang Regime from the southern approaches in order to bring about its surrender. Whenever demanded by future developments the rights of a belligerent will be resorted to against Chungking and hostile concessions taken over.

2. In order to guarantee national security and preservation, the Imperial Government will continue all necessary diplomatic negotiations with reference to the southern regions and also carry out various other plans as may be necessary. In case the diplomatic negotiations break down, preparations for a war with England and America will also be carried forward. First of all, the plans which have been laid with reference to French Indo-China and Thai will be prosecuted, with a view to consolidating our position in the southern territories.

In carrying out the plans outlined in the foregoing article, we will not be deterred by the possibility of being involved in a war with England and America.

3. Our attitude with reference to the German-Soviet War will be based on the spirit of the Tri-Partite Pact. However, we will not enter the conflict for some time but will steadily proceed with military preparations against the Soviet and decide our final attitude independently. At the same time, we will continue carefully correlated activities in the diplomatic field.

. . . In case the German-Soviet War should develop to our advantage, we will make use of our military strength, settle the Soviet question and guarantee the safety of our northern borders. . . .

4. In carrying out the preceding article all plans, especially the use of armed forces, will be carried out in such a way as to place no serious obstacles in the path of our basic military preparations for a war with England and America.

5. In case all diplomatic means fail to prevent the entrance of America into the European War, we will proceed in harmony with our obligations under the Tri-Partite Pact. However, with reference to the time and

method of employing our armed forces we will take independent action.

6. We will immediately turn our attention to placing the nation on a war basis and will take special measures to strengthen the defenses of the nation.

7. Concrete plans covering this program will be drawn up separately.

The main lines of this policy were set and most stubbornly held by the forces who spoke through General Tojo. They did not get their whole way, but a ruinous share of it. They thought that if Japan acquired a self-sufficient base of operation in the south it could wear down China, and stand, if need be, a long war against Britain and the United States. The Army and Navy were to get ready for such a war. But the hope remained that it would not have to be fought. It was expected that if Germany defeated Russia, the United States and Britain would give way; that they would allow Japan to establish the New Order in East Asia at the expense of others.

To Matsuoka this course of action was a rebuff and a mistake. But he buoyed himself up with the belief that his views would prevail later. Thus he busied himself with excuses, assuring Ribbentrop that Japan was preparing for all eventualities and when the time came would turn against Russia; in the meantime the advancing vigil in the Pacific was no less a contribution to the common cause.[25] To Konoye and the Imperial Household the resolution of July 2 was at least a temporary respite from the disputes with which they were surrounded. All gambled on the chance that the German armies would bring both the Soviet Union and the British down before winter came. Then there would be only one strong possible enemy left — the United States. This was the

strategy that failed. But it might have won.

Japan's actions during the next few months followed this plan:

The economic resources of the country were organized for war.

The entry into Indo-China was begun. Before July ended the demands were served upon Petain, and the Japanese Navy and Army moved into Indo-China.

The Army hastened its operational plans against Malaya, Java, and other points in the Netherlands East Indies, Borneo, the Bismarck Archipelago, and the Philippines.[26]

The Navy developed corresponding plans — among them one highly secret tactic. It began to practice the Pearl Harbor attack, conceived first in January. The fleets went into Kagoshima Bay and there the planes practiced coming in low over the mountains, dive bombing, and the use of torpedoes, specially designed for shallow waters.[27]

The Japanese government gave the government of the Soviet Union on July 2 formal assurances that it would observe the neutrality pact.[28] The size of the Kwantung Army was increased (from some 300 thousand men to about twice that number). But troops were withdrawn from the borders of Manchukuo and concentrated at interior points. Orders were given to avoid border trou-

[25] *Ibid.*, Exh. Nos. 636, 796, 1113.

[26] Testimony of General Tanaka (Shinichi), Chief of the Operations Section, General Staff of the Army. The studies were ordered by General Sugiyama, Chief of the General Staff, with the approval of Tojo and General Muto, Chief of the (so-called) Military Affairs Bureau of the War Minister.

[27] Interrogation of Admiral Nagano, *ibid.*, Exh. No. 1127 (a).

[28] When first asked about this by the Soviet Ambassador, Smetanin, on June 25, Matsuoka evaded and left the matter doubtful. Extract from Smetanin's diary, entry for June 25, 1941, *ibid.*, Exh. No. 793.

bles with Russian forces and compose any incidents as quickly as possible.[29] At the same time a new plan of operations against Siberia was prepared; in contrast to former ones it contemplated simultaneous attacks on several fronts.

All these items of preparation looked towards war. And yet most of the Konoye Cabinet still eagerly wished to avoid war with the United States. If persuasion and the use of the least offensive forms could keep the United States quiet, they would not be economized.[30] . . .

The United States and Britain
Prepare to Impose Sanctions

. . . . Each newspaper and each intercept from "Magic" gave further details of the Japanese actions towards Indo-China. By the 12th the American government knew of the demand for bases, to be met by the 20th, under threat of forcible entry.[31] By the 15th it knew the details — eight strategically located air bases and two great naval ports (Camranh and Saigon).[32] These facts, which showed how menacing a position Japan was about to acquire, whetted the wish to end the shipment of war materials. Nomura had little with which to counter the wish. He waited to get orders from the new Foreign Minister, Toyoda — who had taken office on the evening of the 17th (Wash-

ington time). There was an air of baffled pessimism in his presentations.

On the 17th Secretary Hull telephoned to Hamilton from White Sulphur Springs to say that he thought that if it became plain that the new Japanese cabinet intended to stay hooked up with Hitler, the American government should increase its economic and financial restrictions against Japan. But, he added, "always short of being involved in war with Japan.". . .

By July 20 "Magic," as well as other sources, supplied the answers as to whether the reformed Konoye Cabinet would renounce its attachment to Germany or its plan to occupy Indo-China. It did not intend to do either. A message which Toyoda had broadcast on July 19 (Tokyo time) to various Japanese diplomatic missions was intercepted. This stated "that although the Cabinet has changed there will be no departure from the principle that the Tripartite Pact forms the keystone of Japanese national policy." Another intercepted message of July 20 (Tokyo time) revealed that Toyoda told Kato (the Japanese Ambassador in Vichy) that the Japanese Army was ready and would advance into Indo-China on the 24th, whether or not the French government consented. . . .

We Freeze Japan's Funds

On the next day, the 24th, the radio reported that Japanese warships had appeared off Camranh Bay, and that twelve troop transports were on their way south from Hainan. . . .

At eight o'clock in the evening the President's office at Poughkeepsie passed out to the press a release which stated that, in view of the unlimited national emergency, the President was issuing an Executive Order freezing Japanese assets in the United States. "This measure," the

[29] Testimony of General Tanaka.
[30] Testimony of General Tominago (Kijoji), Section Chief, War Ministry, *ibid.*, Exh. No. 705; of General Yanagita (Genzo), Chief, Army Special Service Agency, Harbin, *ibid.*, Exh. No. 723; of General Otsubo (Kazuma), Chief of Staff, Third Front of Kwantung Army, *ibid.*, Exh. No. 837.
[31] This ultimatum date was later changed to 6 p.m., July 22, and then later still to the 24th.
[32] Marshall on July 15 sent a special memorandum to the President calling attention to this "Magic" message, and upon the rescheduling of Japanese merchant shipping under way. *Pearl Harbor Attack,* Part 20, p. 4363.

press release continued, "in effect, brings all financial and import and export trade transactions in which Japanese interests are involved under the control of the government . . ."[33]

The step had been taken which was to force Japan to choose between making terms with us or making war against us. No longer would the United States be providing the resources which left her better able to fight if she should so decide.

On the next morning, the 26th, the requisite official orders were issued.[34] The first quick response within the United States was approval, while the subdued comment in the Japanese press seemed to show dismay. That afternoon, in cabling to Hopkins that he consented to his going to Moscow to see Stalin, the President asked that the Former Naval Person be told that "our concurrent action in regard to Japan is, I think, bearing fruit. I hear their Government is much upset and no conclusive future policy has been determined on."[35] Not much reason can be found for this buoyant note, for in the same cable the President asked that Churchill also be informed that he had as yet received no reply to his suggestion that Indo-China be neutralized, but thought that when it came it probably would be unfavorable. No dew fell from

[33] Press release issued at Poughkeepsie, N. Y., by the White House at 8 p.m., July 25, 1941.
[34] Executive Order, No. 8832, signed by President Roosevelt, July 26, 1941. This amended Executive Order, No. 8389, of April 10, 1940 (as amended) to include Japan and China. Executive Order, No. 8389, prohibited, except when licensed, all transactions: (1) "by, or on behalf of, or pursuant to the direction of any foreign country designated in this Order, or any national thereof." (2) which "involve property in which any foreign country designated in this Order, or any national thereof, has at any time on or since the effective date of this Order had any interest of any nature whatsoever, direct or indirect."
[35] The message is printed in *Pearl Harbor Attack*, Part 20, p. 4373.

"Magic" to freshen the belief that Japan would heed the proposal or the warning.

Events were to show that the freezing order shook the Japanese rulers. But they did not change their course. They were soon to decide to rush full speed ahead, lest they would not have enough oil to reach those distant ports which were marked on the Imperial chart. . . .

The Choice before Japan Is Defined; and Konoye Seeks a Meeting with Roosevelt

The freezing order propelled the Japanese authorities into another urgent round of conferences. All thought that the United States was being wilfully unjust; none advocated that Japan give in. But all, except Tojo and the Army heads, were worried; despite their bitter feeling they were glad to have Konoye keep on trying to change our attitude.

On July 28 the Privy Council met, first alone, and then in the Emperor's presence, to consider the Protocol that had been forced upon the Vichy government for the joint defense of Indo-China. This ruled out Roosevelt's proposal that the country be neutralized. While the Council talked, they could hear power shovels at work around the Imperial Palace, digging shelters. The sounds of war were crossing over the Imperial moat and wall. Old trees, planted when Japan held itself apart, were being dug out to make holes for gun-mounts.

The Cabinet gave the Privy Council the same reasons for the advance into Indo-China as had been given the outside world. It gave no hint of planning any more beyond. But then, as Tojo admitted, the Privy Council when asked to pass upon the resolutions of July 2 had not been told that the government was going to occupy Indo-China by force. In other words these sessions of the Privy Council were only a ceremony, a way of involving all respected Japanese political figures in official decisions. So in this case, by late afternoon the qualms of the Privy Council were met and the agreement with Vichy was unanimously approved.[36]

The real tissue of policy — of peace or war — was treated in talk among Konoye, the Army, and the Navy. The Army, through Tojo, refused to consider any accord with the United States which would limit its freedom to move either north or south. At this very time the Kwantung Army was perfecting its plans for the government of areas in Siberia that were, it was hoped, soon to be taken. The Navy, hitherto a firm negative influence, began to waver.

Admiral Nagano, Chief of the Naval General Staff, was asked by the Emperor to advise as to what course should be followed towards the United States. His answer was a crossroads marker. Japan, he said, should try hard to avert a war with the United States, retiring from its alliance with Germany, if need be. If the effort to adjust relations failed, there would be no other way than to take the initiative in war. One main reason was Japan's need for oil. If the embargo continued all Japanese reserves would be used up in two years. When the Emperor asked whether Japan would win a sweeping victory as in the war with Russia, Nagano said he was doubtful whether Japan would win at all.[37] Kido had intervened to prevent this gloomy report from having too agitating an effect. He advised the Emperor that if Japan annulled the

Tripartite Pact it would earn American contempt, not friendship.

Another opinion was asked of Suzuki, the President of the Planning Board. He was even less hopeful about the stretching of the oil supply. He confirmed the estimate that if the embargo continued, Japan would collapse within two years. . . .[38]

Konoye made up his mind that the only way out of the impasse would be a meeting with Roosevelt. No one, no matter what papers come to light, will be entitled to be sure about his train of purpose. To find a way past both the man of rigid doctrine, Hull, and the hard and threatening Japanese generals; and thus to achieve a compromise that would save both "peace" and "face"? To escape by guile, out of the trap of circumstance in which Japan was caught, now that Germany had failed to release the catch? To gain time and strength for later ventures? . . .

Tojo and the senior Army commanders demanded that the talks with the United States be dropped, and that war be begun as soon as Japanese forces could be placed in position. The Navy called together its senior staff and combat officers at Tokyo. Admiral Yamamoto, the Commander in Chief, explained to them on September 2 that the games about to begin were truly practice for war. The assembled ships rehearsed a series of great battles with the British and American fleets.

As they did, the Prime Minister and Foreign Minister met with the heads of the armed forces every day, and almost every hour every day. Beset, Konoye bent before the demand that the issue between Japan and the United States be faced and forced. He agreed that the Army and Navy should make all dispositions for war. But he struggled for consent to keep

[36] Summary minutes of this meeting are given in *Far East Mil. Trib.*, Exh. Nos. 649, 650. The formal Protocol was supplemented by a letter of July 29, defining in detail the various rights accorded Japan, *ibid.*, Exh. No. 651. They were to be valid as long as the causing circumstances were deemed to exist.

[37] "Kido's Diary," entry for July 31, 1941, and Kido's deposition.

[38] Deposition of Suzuki, *Far East Mil. Trib.*, Exh. No. 3605.

on talking with the United States, while they were doing so. Furthermore, he opposed the naming of any day for the commencement of war.[39]

Konoye won only a short reprieve — six weeks or so more. The argument before which he yielded was that if Japan did not *soon* fight for what it wanted (what he was pledged to get) it would not be able to fight with fair hope of victory, for the defense of its enemies would be too strong and its oil would be short. As later put by General Tojo, the Minister of War, when on trial: "The elasticity in our national power was on the point of extinction."[40]

The cabinet and the High Military Command, having reached agreement on September 4-5, Konoye arranged for a conference before the Throne on the 6th. The program of dual initiative that was prepared for submission to this conference — and adopted by it without change — could only mean war unless there was a reversal in the American attitude. The machinery of war was to be placed in gear; it was to be stopped only if Konoye managed to win American assent to terms which up to then had been rejected.

The first segments of this agenda[41] tell their own story:

1. Determined not to be deterred by the possibility of being involved in a war with America (and England and Holland) in order to secure our national existence, we will proceed with war preparations so that they be completed approximately toward the end of October.

2. At the same time, we will endeavor by every possible diplomatic means to have our demands agreed to by America and England. Japan's minimum demands in these negotiations with America (and England), together with the Empire's maximum concessions are embodied in the attached document.

3. If by the early part of October there is no reasonable hope of having our demands agreed to in the diplomatic negotiations mentioned above, we will immediately make up our minds to get ready for war against America (and England and Holland).

The substance of the most important among Japan's minimum demands can be briefly summarized.

As regards China, the United States and Britain were not to obstruct a settlement along lines specified. They were (presumably as soon as the accord was signed) to close the Burma Road and end help of every kind to the Chiang Kai-shek regime. Japan was to "rigidly adhere" to the right to station troops in various points or areas within China.

As regards current military measures, the United States and Britain were not to establish any bases in the region or increase their Far Eastern forces.

As regards Indo-China, Japan would withdraw when a just peace was made in the Far East, but it was to retain the special relations set down in the agreement which had been forced upon Vichy.

[39] As summed up by General Suzuki, Head of the Planning Board: "The Supreme Command was in favor of making a decision then and there for war; calling off negotiations with the United States; but Konoye opposed, suggesting that no time be set when war was to be commenced, only war preparations." Deposition, *Far East Mil. Trib.*, Exh. No. 3605.

[40] *Ibid.*, Exh. No. 3655.

[41] There are differences of some importance between the text here quoted from Appendix V, "Konoye Memoirs," *Pearl Harbor Attack*, Part

20, pp. 4022-23, and that submitted to the *Far East Mil. Trib.*, Defense Document, No. 1579. The version here given is contained in the text completed by him in the spring of 1942, and carefully reviewed and corrected by him at the time. The other version was turned out with Konoye's consent two years after the war began, and was cut down and revised in part by him. This was printed in Japan. For the history of the several versions and parts of the "Konoye Memoirs," see the testimony of Ushiba (Tomohiko), his private secretary, *ibid.*, Exh. No. 2737.

As regards economic matters, the United States and Britain were to restore trade relations. They were also to engage themselves to see that Japan got the raw materials wanted from the Southwest Pacific.

In return, Japan was to promise not to use Indo-China as a base for southern operations, and to observe the Neutrality Pact with the Soviet Union.

In the event that the United States entered the European war, Japan was to decide independently on the meaning and applicability of the Tripartite Pact.

These were the terms set down by Japan as the price of peace in the Pacific, if not tranquillity. They expressed the same fixed purpose which had taken Japan into Asia years before — to acquire a pliant and self-sustaining empire, to be the "stabilizing" authority throughout the Far East. . . .

The schedule adopted at the Imperial Conference of September 6 was, in Tojo's words, "Initiated by the Imperial High Command and based on its anticipated requirements."[42]

The American Army and Navy were, for reasons explained, seeking time. The Japanese High Command were even more intensely concerned with time, for reverse reasons. They knew that opposed forces in the region, particularly naval and air, could from then on be built up more effectively than their own. They thought that there was only a short season ahead of good fighting weather; after that it would hinder or prevent the kind of operations they planned. And they knew that the reserves of materials for war — particularly oil — would grow less with each day that was allowed to slip by. These were the reasons why they found

long delay intolerable.[43] To them the face of time was getting pock-marked.

Despite every device of economic control, and every twist of diplomacy, the Japanese oil position had not been secured.[44] The total result of all its efforts and outlays was much poorer than Japan hoped or wished. Together natural and synthetic production (Inner Zone of Japan) in 1941 provided only some 3 million barrels, or 10 to 12 per cent of Japan's estimated minimum needs.[45] The other 30 to 35 million barrels, the other 90 per cent, had been obtained from the United States, the Caribbean, and the Indies.[46]

The Japanese government during the thirties had imported far more than required for current use. Much had been put into reserve. Towards the end of 1939, the reserve stock had been highest — about 55 million barrels, enough to last a year and a half or longer. But thereafter use — especially for military operations and training — had grown, while it had

---

[42] Defense deposition, General Tojo. *Far East Mil. Trib.*, Exh. No. 3655.

[43] See, in particular, "Konoye's Memoirs" and the defense depositions of General Tojo, General Tanaka, Chief of the Operations Section of the General Staff, and Marquis Kido.

[44] The civilian consumption of motor gasoline, for example, was cut from some 6 to 7 million barrels per annum in the past to 1.6 million in 1941. The tanker fleet was increased from 230 thousand tons in 1937 to about 575 thousand tons at the end of 1941.

[45] These estimated needs were indeed minimum both for any training period for war, or for war. They allowed for almost no civilian consumption of gasoline, and greatly reduced amounts of fuel oil.

[46] Japanese imports had been (in millions of barrels for fiscal years beginning April 1):

	Crude Oil	Refined Products	Total
1931	6.4	13.3	19.7
1935	12.8	20.6	33.5
1937	20.2	16.6	36.9
1939	18.8	11.8	30.6
1940	22.0	15.1	37.1

become much harder to import. The reserve had shrunk — probably to less than 50 million barrels by September 1941.[47] The fuel oil stocks held by the Navy had shrunk from some 29 million to some 22 million. But the reserve of aviation gasoline had been increased from 1 million barrels to about 4 million; the early American hindrance had been completely overcome. The inflow from both the Western Hemisphere and the Indies was at an end. Japan could no longer draw propelling energy from the countries whose position and safety were under threat.[48] If Japan was to fight, the longer it waited the greater the risk that the battle might be

Of which total the following portion came from the United States:

1937 about 29 million barrels, about 80 per cent
1939 " 26 " " " 85 " "
1940 " 23 " " " 60 " "

Totals of Japanese imports are derived from reports of the United States Strategic Bombing Survey, those of American exports from unpublished statistics of the Bureau of Foreign and Domestic Commerce. The latter include the figures for crude oil, gasoline, and other oil motor fuels, gas, fuel and residual fuel oil, and lubricating oil. Owing to the time interval between import and export entries and other factors, these estimates are only approximate.

[47] These estimates of reserves (in the so-called Inner Zone of Japan) are derived from the figures contained in the reports of the United States Strategic Bombing Survey. However, in a memorandum submitted by the President of the Planning Board to the Liaison Conference of September 3, 1941, total reserve stocks were put at 52.8 million barrels.

The Survey in its report — *Oil in Japan's War*, p. 10 — estimated that at the time of Pearl Harbor stocks had fallen to about 43 million barrels.

[48] The record of decline in American exports to Japan was (in millions of barrels):

Last five	Crude Petroleum	Gasoline	Gas and Fuel Oil	Residual Fuel Oil	Lubricating Oil
months 1939	6.7	0.5	2.8	1.3	0.3
1940	5.2	2.7	2.0	0.8	0.6
1941	0.1	0.1	0.2	.0	.0

Unpublished statistics of Bureau of Foreign and Domestic Commerce.

lost for lack of oil or other essential raw materials. So the oil gauge influenced the time of decision.

Not only the time of decision, but the war plans. The wish to obtain economic reserves for a long war was an important factor in determining the spheres to be occupied. It was decided by Imperial Military Headquarters that to be sure of enough oil, rubber, rice, bauxite, iron ore, it was necessary to get swift control of Java, Sumatra, Borneo, and Malaya. In order to effect the occupation and protect the transport lines to Japan, it was necessary to expel the United States from the Philippines, Guam, and Wake, and Britain from Singapore. Thus it can be said that the points of attack and occupation were settled by placing these vital raw material needs alongside of the estimate of Japan's military means. And having settled these, the question of the weather entered in to hurry the final action.[49]

The Army and Navy feared even to see two, three, or four *months* elapse. For on their strategic calendar October and November were the best months for landing operations. December was possible but difficult, January or later, impossible.[50] If the plan were to include an attack

[49] This brief comment on the way in which the wish to obtain economic reserves affected the plans with which Japan began the war is drawn from several studies made available to me by the Military Intelligence Division of the Supreme Headquarters of the Allied Command in Tokyo; especially the information furnished by Colonel Hattori (Takushiro), former Chief of the Operations Section of the General Staff of the Japanese Army. It corresponds also to the explanations of Admiral Toyoda (Soemu), former Commanding Officer, Kure Naval District.

[50] Tojo deposition, *Far East Mil. Trib.*, Exh. No. 3655. As stated by Admiral Shimada, Minister of the Navy, in his deposition, Exh. No. 3565: "With the advent of December, northeasterly monsoons would blow with force in the Formosan Straits, the Philippines, and Malayan areas rendering military operations difficult."

on Pearl Harbor by the Great Circle Route, navigational and weather conditions would, it was judged, become unfavorable after January.[51] Furthermore the sooner the southern operations were under way, the less the chance that the Soviet Union could attack from the north; if they could be completed before the end of winter, that danger need not be feared.[52]

Thus, leaving Konoye to go on with his talks with the United States, the Army and Navy threw themselves at once into the plans for action. The Operations Section of the Army began to get ready to capture Malaya, Java, Borneo, the Bismarck Archipelago, the Indies, and the Philippines; it was to be fully ready by the end of October. The Navy finished its war games. These included the surprise attack on Pearl Harbor and the American fleet there. At the end of the games the two general staffs conferred on the result and found it satisfactory.[53]

By the end of September these steps towards war — if diplomacy should fail — were well under way. Still Konoye and Toyoda found themselves reading the unchanging reports of American resistance. The President was still in the White House — planning to go no further than Warm Springs. Hull and his draftsmen were still dissecting every document which came from Tokyo with the scalpel of mistrust. In his apartment in the Wardman Park Hotel there seemed to be no sense of hurry. No calendar hung there with October ringed in red.

Time had become the meter of strategy for both governments. But one did not mind its passing, while the other was crazed by the tick of the clock. . . .

The world may long wonder what would have happened had the President agreed then to meet with Konoye. Grew and Dooman, at the time and later, had a sense that the refusal was a sad error. To them it seemed that the American government had missed a real chance to lead Japan back to peaceful ways. Konoye, they thought, was sincere in his acceptance of those principles of international conduct for which the American government stood, and with the support of the Emperor would be able to carry through his promises. In words which Grew confided to his diary:

It is my belief that the Emperor, the Government of Prince Konoye and the militant leaders of Japan (the leaders then in control) had come to accept the status of the conflict in China, in conjunction with our freezing measures and Japan's economic condition as evidence of failure or comparative incapacity to succeed.

Our attitude, he thought (and others since have thought the same), showed a lack both of insight and suppleness, if not of desire. The mistake sprang, in this view, from failure to appreciate why Konoye could not be as clear and conclusive as the American government wished; and to admit that Japan could correct its course only in a gradual and orderly way. Wise American statesmanship, thus,

[51] This forecast of weather conditions was borne out by the event — in early December. "The start (for the attack on Pearl Harbor) was from Saeki, the training harbor, about November 17, 1941; then north and across the Pacific, just south of the Aleutians, then south to Pearl Harbor. We had studied this route for a long time. Upon returning we suffered from heavy seas and strong winds." Interrogation of Captain Watanabe, on Admiral Yamamoto's staff.

[52] As stated by General Tojo in his defense deposition, and by Colonel Hattori in his study for the Supreme Command of the Allied Powers.

[53] See evidence of records of Admiral Nagano and Admiral Yamamoto, Commander in Chief of the Combined Fleet, *ibid.*, Exh. Nos. 1126 and 1127. For interesting details, see Captain Ellis M. Zacharias, *Secret Missions* (New York [1946]), pp. 243, *et seq.*

would have bartered adjustment for adjustment, agreeing to relax our economic restraints little by little as Japan, little by little, went our way. Instead, the judgment ends, it was dull and inflexible. By insisting that Japan promise in black and white, then and there, to conform to every American requirement, it made Konoye's task impossible.

It will be always possible to think that Grew was correct; that the authorities in Washington were too close to their texts and too soaked in their disbelief to perceive what he saw. That the American government was as stern as a righteous schoolmaster cannot be denied. Nor that it was unwilling either to ease Japanese failure, or to provide any quick or easy way to improve their hard lot. But the records since come to hand do not support the belief that a real chance of maintaining peace in the Pacific — on or close to the terms for which we had stood since 1931 — was missed. They do not confirm the opinion that Konoye was prepared, without reserve or trickery, to observe the rules set down by Hull.[54] Nor that he would have been able to do so, even though a respite was granted and he was allowed to grade the retreat gently.

If Konoye was ready and able — as Grew thought — to give Roosevelt trustworthy and satisfactory promises of a new sort, he does not tell of them in his "Memoirs." Nor has any other record

[54] For example, the decisions in regard to China. How reconcile two of Hull's principles (those stipulating non-intervention in domestic affairs and respect for the integrity and independence of China) with the terms specified on September 6 and reaffirmed by a Liaison Conference of September 13, as "Magic" revealed? China was to be required to assent to the stationing of Japanese Army units "for a necessary period" in prescribed areas in Inner Mongolia and North China, and for the stationing of Japanese warships and military units in Hainan, Amoy, and other localities. There was to be a Sino-Japanese economic coalition.

available to me disclosed them. He was a prisoner, willing or unwilling, of the terms precisely prescribed in conferences over which he presided. The latest of these were the minimum demands specified by the Imperial Conference of September 6, just reviewed. It is unlikely that he could have got around them or that he would have in some desperate act discarded them. The whole of his political career speaks to the contrary.

In proof of his ability to carry out his assurances, Konoye stressed first, that his ideas were approved by the Army and Navy; and second, that senior officials (Vice-Chiefs of Staff) of both branches would accompany him on his mission. If and when he said "Yes," they would say "Yes"; and thus the United States could count upon unified execution of any accord. But it seems to me far more likely that the Army and Navy had other thoughts in mind on assigning high officials to go along with him. They would be there to see that Konoye did not yield to the wish for peace or the will of the President. The truer version of the bond is expressed in the title of one of the subsections of Konoye's "Memoirs": "The Independence of the Supreme Command and State Affairs from Each Other: The Anguish of Cabinets from Generation to Generation."

Konoye could have honestly agreed that Japan would stop its southern advance and reduce its forces in China to the minimum needed to assure compliance with its wishes. That is really all. To the seekers of the New Order in East Asia this seemed much; to the American government it seemed too little. The error, the fault, in American policy — if there was one — was not in the refusal to trust what Konoye could honestly offer. It was in insisting that Japan entirely clear out of Indo-China and China (and perhaps out of Manchukuo) and give up all exclusive privileges in these countries.

In any case, the President and Hull were convinced that Konoye's purposes were murky and his freedom of decision small. Therefore they concluded that to meet with him before Japan proved its intentions would be a great mistake.[55] It could bring confusion into both American policies and our relations with the other opponents of the Axis. So Grew's earnest appeal for a daring try did not influence the responses to Japan that Hull's drafting squad was putting together. They took nothing that came from Tokyo for granted; wanted everything shown. The Army and Navy were both saying that they could use well all the time they could get. Both Stimson and Knox approved "stringing out negotiations." But neither wanted Roosevelt to meet Konoye or to soften American terms just to gain time.[56]

Hull was guided by these thoughts in the prepared answer which he gave Nomura on October 2, the answer on which the plans of Japan hung. The Japanese proposals (of September 6), this said in effect, did not provide a basis for a settlement, and were on essential points ambiguous.[57] The meeting between the President and Konoye was put off till there was a real meeting of minds about the application of the four principles — which were the essential foundations of proper relations.

Upon reading this, the opinion nurtured by Konoye and Toyoda, that Japanese and American terms could be reconciled, dropped. This, the note of October 2, rather than the one of November 26 on which controversy has centered, ended the era of talk. For the crisis that followed in Japan brought into power a group determined to fight us rather than move further our way. Thereafter war came first, diplomacy second....

The American government, while talking with Japan, could not forget that it was allied with Germany and Italy. American planes and warships were now providing watch and ward over wide areas of the Middle and Western Atlantic and around Iceland.[58] Encounters were becoming frequent. On September 11 the President, having discussed his words with Hull, Stimson, and Knox, broadcast: "The aggression is not ours. Ours is solely defense. But let this warning be clear. From now on, if German or Italian vessels of war enter the waters, the protection of which is necessary for American defense, they do so at their own peril. The orders which I have given as Commander-in-Chief of the United States Army and Navy are to carry out that policy — at once."[59]

---

[55] Ott's judgment of the prospect was at the time the same as that reached by the American government. He thought that even though certain circles about Konoye genuinely sought a *détente* with the United States, the effort was certain to fail in the end. He reported that the purpose of Konoye's mission was being pictured to the Navy and activist circles as a last step to convince the Japanese people that a peaceful settlement was not possible. Acceptance of the American terms would, Ott predicted, swiftly result in grave inner convulsions. (See Most Urgent telegram, Ott to Ribbentrop, September 4, 1941. *Far East Mil. Trib.*, Exh. No. 801A.)

[56] Stimson diary, entry for October 6, 1941.

[57] The text is to be found in *Foreign Relations: Japan*, II, 656, *et seq.*

[58] On August 25 Atlantic fleet forces were ordered to destroy surface raiders which attacked shipping along sea lanes between North America and Iceland, or which approached these lanes sufficiently closely to threaten such shipping. On September 3 the Western Atlantic area of operations covered by the United States Atlantic fleet was extended eastward. These were changes, Nos. 2 and 4, to W.P.L. 51. *Pearl Harbor Attack*, Part 5, p. 2295.

[59] While this speech was in preparation, the President had the impulse to be more explicit in his statements but Hull warned against any reference to shooting.

On September 26 the Navy issued orders to protect all ships engaged in commerce in our defensive waters — by patrolling, covering, escorting, reporting, or destroying German and Italian naval, land, and air forces encountered.[60] As the President wrote to Mackenzie King, Prime Minister of Canada, ". . . we have begun to have practically sole charge of the safety of things to twenty-six degrees longitude, and to a further extension in the waters well to the eastward of Iceland."[61]

Further, it was foreseen that before long American merchant ships, manned by American crews, would soon be making the whole voyage to Britain. By the end of September, agreement had been reached between the President and Congressional leaders that the Neutrality Act should be so amended as to permit American merchant ships to enter combat areas and the ports of belligerents. The President's message so recommending was sent to Congress October 8.

Would this bring war with Germany? Hull did not think so; Hitler would not, he thought, declare a war as a result of any action of ours unless he thought it to his own advantage.[62] But should this turn out to be wrong, how would Japan con-

strue its obligations under Article III of the Tripartite Pact? It was not possible to deduce a reliable answer from either the Japanese talk or texts. The American government sought to have Japan, in some form or other, cancel the obligation. The Konoye Cabinet lived in an agony of division over the issue. Unwilling to separate from Germany, but equally unwilling to lose a chance for a settlement with the United States, it fell into bigamous vows.

Formula after formula was served up to Washington. None was a conclusive repudiation of the tie. The American government was asked to feel safe with the assurance that Japan would construe its obligation independently. This was accompanied by covert hints that we need not fear the decision, if other matters were amiably adjusted. Thus on September 18, Ushiba, Konoye's secretary, said to Dooman that it was impossible for Japan to go farther than the formula already offered on the Tripartite Pact before the besought Konoye-Roosevelt meeting. "He added, however, that an understanding had been reached among the various influential elements in Japan which would enable Prince Konoye to give orally and directly to the President an assurance with regard to the attitude of Japan which, he felt sure, would be entirely satisfactory to the President."[63]

The German government was doing all it could to induce Japan to be faithful. It asked public reaffirmation of Matsuoka's version of the pact — that, in the event of war between Germany and the United States, Japan would join Germany. A deciphered cable sent by Oshima with a special request that it be shown to the Army and Navy related what Ribbentrop was saying: that the whole Ger-

[60] This was Western Hemisphere Defense Plan, No. 5 (W.P.L. 52), effective October 11, 1941.
[61] Letter, Roosevelt to King, September 27, 1941. Churchill understood these orders to mean that American ships would attack any Axis ships found in the prohibited zone and assume responsibility for all fast British convoys other than troop convoys between America and Iceland. See his message to General Smuts of September 14, 1941. Churchill, *The Grand Alliance*, p. 517.
[62] The event proved Hull to be correct. On September 17 the German Navy asked Hitler to change its orders to permit, among other things, attacks on escorting forces in any operational area at any time. Hitler decided against such action for the time being, until the outcome of the fighting in Russia was decided, which he expected soon. *Fuehrer Conferences*, 1941, II, 33.

[63] *Foreign Relations: Japan*, II, 628.

man government was displeased with the Japanese attitude and secrecy; and that if Japan took a "wishy-washy" attitude and proceeded with the talks without consulting Germany there was no telling what Germany might do.[64] Another deciphered cable made it clear that the Japanese government, while seeking to soothe Berlin, refused to do as asked. Oshima was told that just as German policy had been governed by German aims, so Japanese policy would be guided by Japanese aims; that the original purpose of the Tripartite Pact was to restrain the United States from entering the war, and this was still Japan's purpose.[65]

Thus the American government could gather that devotion to Germany probably would not stand in the way of an accord that Japan found desirable. But it did not want to buy off the threat. Nor to have to rely on secret demi-promises. It wanted the connection dissolved. As long as Japan refused to do so, its appeals to be believed were not in good standing. It was thought to be — it had to be — corrupted by evil association. Thus the Axis connection, courted in the first months of his Ministry, was one of the causes of the tragic dilemma in which Konoye now found himself. . . .

On November 5, the same day that the Japanese government decided to go to war if its final proposals (A or B) were rejected, Stark and Marshall (with Chiang Kai-shek's appeal before them) summed up their judgment of the line to be held. Their memorandum to the President advised that:

(a) The basic military policies and strategy agreed to in the United States — British Staff conversations remain sound. The primary objective of the two nations is the defeat of Germany. If Japan be defeated and Germany remain undefeated, decision will still have not been reached. In any case, an unlimited offensive war should not be undertaken against Japan, since such a war would greatly weaken the combined effort in the Atlantic against Germany, the most dangerous enemy.

(b) War between the United States and Japan should be avoided while building up defensive forces in the Far East, until such time as Japan attacks or directly threatens territories whose security to the United States is of very great importance. Military action against Japan should be undertaken only in one or more of the following contingencies: (1) A direct act of war by Japanese armed forces against the territory or mandated territory of the United States, the British Commonwealth, or the Netherlands East Indies; (2) The movement of Japanese armed forces into Thailand to the West of 100° East, or South of 10° North; or into Portuguese Timor, New Caledonia, or the Loyalty Islands.[66]

(d) Considering world strategy, a Japanese advance against Kunming, into Thailand except as previously indicated, or an attack on Russia would not justify intervention by the United States against Japan.

(e) All possible aid short of actual war against Japan should be extended to the Chinese Central Government.

Specifically, they recommend:

That the dispatch of United States armed forces for intervention against Japan in China be disapproved.

That material aid to China be accelerated consonant with the needs of Russia, Great Britain, and our own forces.

That aid to the American Volunteer Group be continued and accelerated to the maximum practicable extent.

That no ultimatum be delivered to Japan.[67]

---

[64] Telegram, No. 1198, Oshima to Toyoda, October 1, 1941.

[65] Telegram, No. 873, Toyoda to Oshima, October 8, 1941.

[66] The thought was that any movement of this kind would be a plan to go into the Gulf of Siam, on the way to attack the Malay-Kra Peninsula.

[67] *Pearl Harbor Attack*, Part 14, pp. 1061–62.

The President followed this traced line. On the 6th he told Stimson that he might propose a truce in which there would be no movement of armed forces for six months, during which China and Japan might come to terms. Stimson wanted time also but objected to this means of getting it. The movement of forces to the Philippines, he thought, should not be halted. And the Chinese, in his opinion, should not be left alone with the Japanese; they would, he correctly forecast, balk at any such arrangement.[68] The President placed the idea of a truce aside, but not far.

On this next day, November 7, the President asked the cabinet for advice. All agreed with a statement made by Hull that the situation was extremely serious and that Japan might attack at any time. The position being maintained in the talks with Japan was approved; the current program for the extension of military forces in the Southwest Pacific area was endorsed; the cohesion between our own activities in that area and those of Britain, Australia, and the Indies was noted with satisfaction. Thus it was decided to "carry on," and to leave Japan to decide whether to turn about or attack. The President took a poll, asking whether the people would back the government up if it struck at Japan in case it attacked English or Dutch territories in the Pacific. All the cabinet was of the opinion that it would. It was agreed that speeches should be made to acquaint the country with the situation.[69]

In the evening after this cabinet meeting Nomura paid his first call on Hull since the advent of the Tojo Cabinet. Earnestly he presented Proposal A and asked a quick answer. Hull, after a rapid glance at the contents (which he already knew) indicated his attitude by observing what a wonderful chance Japan had to launch forth on a real new order which would gain it moral leadership in the Far East.

Nomura asked to talk to the President, and was received on the 10th. He had an invisible naval escort not of his own choosing. Not many hours before he entered the White House, his former colleague, Vice-Admiral Nagumo, on board the aircraft carrier *Akagi*, issued Striking Force Operations Order, No. 1. All ships in this force were directed to complete battle preparations by November 20, and to assemble in Hitokappu Bay, Etorofu Island, Kuriles. This was the force that was to attack Pearl Harbor.

Nomura did not know either the schedule or geography written in this order, one of many placing the Japanese Navy in location for war. But he knew that he was in a race with such orders, and that only some miracle of conversion could stop them. The smoke was over the funnels. Thus he pleaded for acceptance of what he came to offer on the ground that Japan was doing all it could in the light of reason and of history. But his two American listeners were unmoved. Their books, open and secret, contained the record of Japan's desertion of the ways of peace and order.

The President met the plea by saying, in substance, that Japan should prove its intentions by actions, prove them by beginning to move its troops out of China and Indo-China.[70] This answer could hardly have surprised Nomura. For on the evening before the Postmaster General, Walker, had said to him, "I tell this only to you, swearing to God. Both our

---

[68] Stimson diary, entry for November 6, 1941.

[69] *Ibid.*, entry for November 7, and the written statement by Hull, *Pearl Harbor Attack*, Part 2, p. 429.

[70] Hull's memorandum of this important talk is printed in *Foreign Relations: Japan*, II, 715–19.

'boss' and the Secretary of State have received an authentic report that Japan has decided a policy of taking action."[71] Nomura had not contradicted.

Proposal A thus died; it was, in truth, dead before it was delivered.

The speeches meant to awaken the American people to the crisis were delivered (on November 11) by Secretary of the Navy Knox and Welles. But at the same time a last, harried effort was begun to find some way to keep war from coming. Kurusu was on his way; and with his arrival, it was known, the last act would begin, the act that would end with peace or war. . . .

Nomura placed Proposal B before Hull on November 20. The English text, as cabled some days before, had been intercepted and read. Hull knew that it was regarded in Tokyo as the last bargain; the hinge on the breech of the cannon.

There were five numbered points on the white piece of paper which Nomura gave to Hull. They have been printed in many other places, but I think the reader will want them before him as he follows the narrative:

1. Both the Government of Japan and the United States undertake not to make any armed advancement into any of the regions in the South-eastern Asia and the Southern Pacific area excepting the part of French Indo-China where the Japanese troops are stationed at present.

2. The Japanese Government undertakes to withdraw its troops now stationed in French Indo-China upon either the restoration of peace between Japan and China or the establishment of an equitable peace in the Pacific area.

In the meantime the Government of Japan declares that it is prepared to remove its troops now stationed in the southern part of French Indo-China to the northern part of the said territory upon the conclusion of the present arrangement which shall later be embodied in the final agreement.

3. The Government of Japan and the United States shall cooperate with a view to securing the acquisition of those goods and commodities which the two countries need in Netherlands East Indies.

4. The Government of Japan and the United States mutually undertake to restore their commercial relations to those prevailing prior to the freezing of the assets.

The Government of the United States shall supply Japan a required quantity of oil.

5. The Government of the United States undertakes to refrain from such measures and actions as will be prejudicial to the endeavors for the restoration of general peace between Japan and China."[72]

Whoever insisted on the last paragraph — Tojo and the Army certainly did — insisted on war.

Hull glanced over the text to make sure it was the same as that which was known. It was. Then, on two points in particular, he spoke out. Linking Japan's treatment of China to Hitler's actions, he defended our aid to China. Kurusu remarked that perhaps this point (No. 5) in the Japanese terms might be construed to mean that the United States would end its help only at the time when talks between Japan and China would have started. Hull also dwelt on the fact that this truce would leave Japan a full member of the Axis pact, and hence still a potential enemy of the United States and Great Britain. To this Kurusu had no answer.[73]

Hull found no dissent, either within the State Department or at the White House, to his opinion that the proposal was "clearly unacceptable." His reasons for finding it so are summed up again in his "Memoirs":

[71] Nomura manuscript (op. cit.), entry for November 9, 1941. The Ambassador transmitted a report of this talk with Walker to Tokyo on the 10th.

[72] Foreign Relations: Japan, II, 755–56.
[73] Ibid., II, 753–55.

The commitments we should have to make were virtually a surrender. We on our part should have to supply Japan as much oil as she might require, suspend our freezing measures, and resume full commercial relations with Tokyo. We should have to discontinue aid to China and withdraw our moral and material support from the recognized Chinese Government of Chiang Kai-shek. We should have to help Japan obtain products of the Netherlands East Indies. We should have to cease augmenting our military forces in the western Pacific.

Japan, on her part, would still be free to continue her military operations in China, to attack the Soviet Union, and to keep her troops in northern Indo-China until peace was effected with China. . . . Japan thus clung to her vantage point in Indo-China which threatened countries to the south and vital trade routes.

The President and I could only conclude that agreeing to these proposals would mean condonement by the United States of Japan's past aggressions, assent to future courses of conquest by Japan, abandonment of the most essential principles of our foreign policy, betrayal of China and Russia, and acceptance of the role of silent partner aiding and abetting Japan in her effort to create a Japanese hegemony over the western Pacific and eastern Asia.[74]

Inspection of such Japanese records as I have seen leaves room for doubt about some features of this judgment. It is not certain that the meaning which Hull attached to some of the points in Proposal B is the necessary meaning; or that his total estimate of the Japanese offer to begin to retreat was just. Perhaps so, probably so, but not surely so.

It would be a barren exercise, I think, now to re-examine, feature by feature, the face and soul of this last Japanese formula for peace. The result would be inconclusive; for even its authors were divided and mixed up in their intentions. And even a less suspicious reading would

have, I think, led to the same rejection. For the situation had grown too immense and entangled for haggling. Japan had forced the creation of a defensive coalition more vast than the empire of the Pacific for which it plotted. This was not now to be quieted by a temporary halt along the fringe of the Japanese advance.

Acceptance of this Japanese proposal would have imperilled the trustful unity of the coalition. As the next few days were to show, China would have felt itself deserted, if not betrayed. Elsewhere the will to carry on the fight against Germany without pause or compromise might have been corrupted. The Japanese Army and Navy would have been left in place to take advantage of any future weakness.

Even — to carry conjecture further — if the American government had taken these risks and entered into this accord, there would have been war in the Pacific. For it seems to me almost certain that the truce would have broken down as soon as signed. Quarrels would have started over the military movements in which both sides were engaged. Japan would not have ceased its preparations for attack. Nor can it be thought that we or the British would have ended the movement of planes and ships and anti-aircraft and radar to the Philippines and Malaya. Each side would have thought the other to be taking advantage of the truce.

If these disputes did not bring the truce to a quick end, arguments over oil would have done so. Very different notions existed in Tokyo and Washington as to what was expected under the phrase "a required quantity of oil." The Japanese government had told Nomura to let us know before signing how much it had in mind. It wanted four million tons a year from the United States, and one million tons a year from the Indies.[75] The Ameri-

[74] Hull, *op. cit.*, II, 1069–70.

[75] One million according to the intercepted telegram from Togo to Nomura, No. 833, sent from

can government would not have agreed to supply anything like such quantities, which were enough to keep Japanese reserves intact.

In sum, the paper given by Nomura to Hull on November 20 would have marked only the start of new disputes, not the end of old ones. . . .

War might be in the secret messages; it might be in the nerves; but the wish to avoid it was still alive. Hull began to compound a counter-offer to Proposal B which might defer the climax without giving Japan an advantage, or destroying the faith of our allies. The drafting squad ransacked the files for old memoranda, and drew upon a refreshingly new one from the Treasury. . . .

The very making of the offer seemed likely to have troublesome, if not ruinous, effects. It would be self-defeating to give a true and full explanation to the American people. A confused domestic debate was apt to follow and be in full flow when the war crisis came. More worrisome still was the prospect that, despite whatever was said, the other nations fighting the Axis would feel let down. There was no time to convince Chiang Kai-shek that China would not suffer and would not be deserted.[76] The other members of the coalition were showing themselves luke-warm — not opposing the truce, but not welcoming it. Was it, as Hull averred, only a maneuver, or was it a wavering in the ranks?

Sometime during the night of the 25th, Churchill's answer to the President ar-

rived.[77] It left the American government free to do what it thought best, but seemed to fall in with the view that a truce with Japan was unfair to China. Doubt seemed to overrule enthusiasm. The text is given so that the reader may judge for himself:[78]

Most Secret for the President from the Former Naval Person. "Your message about Japan received tonight. Also full accounts from Lord Halifax of discussions and your counter project to Japan on which Foreign Secretary has sent some comments. Of course, it is for you to han-dle this business and we certainly do not want an additional war. There is only one point that disquiets us. What about Chiang Kai-shek? Is he not having a very thin diet? Our anxiety is about China. If they collapse our joint dangers would enormously increase. We are sure that

[77] There is a conflict of report as to when this cable or its substance was known to the President and Hull. According to the time stamps on the face of the original, it was sent from London at 6 a.m. on November 26, received by the code room of the State Department at 12:55 a.m., November 26, which is before the time of dis-patch, allowance being made for five hours' time difference. It also carries the notation that it was sent over to the White House at 9:05 a.m., on the 26th.

But two of the participants in the afternoon and evening meetings with Hull on the 25th have the remembered impression that either the cable or the substance of it was known to them then; they recall even Hull's comments that Churchill's message did not seem to agree entirely with Eden's. Despite the absence of any record, it is possible that the substance of this message was transmitted earlier in the day through the British Embassy in Washington or some other channel. Hull's reference to this point in his book (*op. cit.*, II, 1081) can be read either way, but suggests that Hull knew its contents on the night of the 25th.

[78] In the minute that Churchill sent to Eden on November 23 he indicated favor towards the counterproposal being prepared by the State De-partment, provided the United States and Britain remained free to continue their aid to China. But on this point he found the draft which Hull sub-mitted inadequate. Churchill, *The Grand Alli-ance*, pp. 595–96.

Tokyo on November 26. These figures were, the Foreign Minister said, to be taken as the basis of negotiation and were not the absolute minimum. *Pearl Harbor Attack*, Part 12, p. 177. Other Japanese documents put the amount to be asked of the Indies at two million tons. *Far East Mil. Trib.*, Exh. No. 2944.

[76] The intercepted message, No. 821, from Togo to Nomura on the 24th read in part: ". . . our demand for a cessation of aid to Chiang . . . is a most essential condition." *Loc. cit.*

the regard of the United States for the Chinese cause will govern your action. We feel that the Japanese are most unsure of themselves."[79]

Hull, in the course of the night, added up the sum of pros and cons. The reason for going ahead with the counterproposal had come to seem unreal. What we had to offer, it was all but certain, would not buy even time. The objections seemed many and hard to meet. He decided to discard it and let events take their course. The verdict was reached after tormenting uncertainty. But once reached, a calm sense followed that he had done all that a man could do. . . .

The long Ten-Point Memorandum on principles, which was our response to Proposal B, was received in Tokyo on the morning of the 27th. Along with it Nomura and Kurusu sent a convoy of troubled comment. They thought the answer hard and dumbfounding. But they found nothing in it compelling Japan to resort to war. They were afraid, as "Magic" let Washington know, that the United States and Britain might try to forestall Japan by occupying the Indies, thus bringing on war. Even this late, Nomura advised his government to keep on with the effort to reach a peaceful accord. He recalled a remark the President had made in an earlier talk — that there would be "no last words."[80] But, he added, if his counsel was not taken, it would be best not to keep up a false front of friendliness, and to strike from behind it. Kurusu, also, tried to be calming. He attributed our statement in part to knowledge of the Japanese military movements and concentrations in the south.[81]

Another Liaison Conference was called as soon as the American paper was read (November 27). This summarily dismissed our statement of principles as a humiliating ultimatum. It was resolved to proceed with the program adopted on November 5; that is, to go to war as soon as the striking forces were in position. Stratagem had failed. Force would be used. Japan would do or die.

As was natural, the men who made this decision pleaded later that it was compelled by the terms placed upon peace by the United States. Thus, the former Foreign Minister, Togo, one of the more conciliatory members of the government, argued that "Japan was now asked not only to abandon all the gains of her years of sacrifice, but to surrender her international position as a power in the Far East. That surrender, as he saw it, would have amounted to national suicide. The only way to face this challenge and defend ourselves was war."[82]

This was not a valid attitude. The idea that compliance with the American terms would have meant "extinction" for Japan, or so deeply hurt it that it could not guard its just interests, is an absurdity. Japan was not asked to give up any land or resources except those which it held by force of arms. Its independence was not in peril. Its Army, Navy, and Air Force would have remained in being. Its chances to trade with the rest of the world would have been restored. Its struggle against the extension of communism could have combined with that of China and the West. Extinction threatened the plan for expansion in Asia, but not Japan or the Japanese.

[79] *Pearl Harbor Attack*, Part 14, p. 1300.

[80] Intercepted Telegrams, Nos. 1180, 1189, and 1190, Nomura to Togo, November 26, 1941, set forth the Ambassador's views at length.

[81] Telegram, No. 1206, Nomura to Togo, November 27, and memorandum of telephone conversation between Kurusu and Yamamoto on November 27th.

[82] Togo deposition, *Far East Mil. Trib.*, Exh. No. 3646.

Charles A. Beard: APPEARANCES AND REALITIES

Secret War Decisions and Plans

THERE is also now available sufficient evidence respecting two primary questions with which my inquiry is particularly concerned: (1) How did the secret actions of the Roosevelt Administration bearing on relations with Japan from August 17 to December 7, 1941, as described in official documents now available, square with official representations of the Administration to the American people at the time — realities with appearances? (2) Do these official documents sustain the official thesis respecting relations with Japan presented to Congress and the people by President Roosevelt's message to Congress on December 8, 1941?

On that occasion, the President said — to repeat, for convenience — that on December 7, 1941, the United States was at peace with Japan, that at the solicitation of Japan it was still in conversation with the Japanese Government and Emperor, looking toward the maintenance of peace in the Pacific, and that on that day Japan had undertaken a planned "surprise offensive," of which the attack on Pearl Harbor was a phase. Did the course of American-Japanese affairs as conducted during the months preceding Pearl Harbor, however it "looked," actually point in the direction of peace with Japan? Were those affairs in such a state at any time during this period that the President actually expected them to eventuate in the maintenance of peace in the Pacific? Did the Japanese Government make any proposals during this period which looked to the possibility of maintaining peace in the Pacific? And, if so, how did Secretary Hull and President Roosevelt treat these proposals with a view to the maintenance of peace? Did the President think that the Japanese final memorandum delivered to Secretary Hull on December 7 actually constituted no threat or hint of an armed attack? Was the Japanese offensive really a surprise to the Administration? With reference to these questions there are some answers in the documents now available.

As early as October 8, 1940, during the campaign of that year while he was still making peace pledges to the country, President Roosevelt had become convinced that Japan would make a mistake and that the United States would enter a war in the Pacific. He expressed this conviction to Admiral J. O. Richardson, Commander in Chief of the Fleet in the Pacific, whose duty it was to prepare plans for the war thus foretold by the President.[1] The development of an American war plan, based on arrangements made with the British Commonwealth and the Netherlands in the spring of 1941, contemplated a general war in which the United States would participate when and if it came[2] — a plan which President Roosevelt approved, "except officially," to use Admiral Stark's ingenious phrase.

On December 14, 1940, the American Ambassador in Tokyo, Joseph Grew, wrote a long letter to President Roosevelt on American-Japanese relations, in the course of which he said that, unless the

[1] See above, p. 416.

[2] See above, pp. 442 ff.

From *President Roosevelt and the Coming of the War, 1941* by Charles A. Beard (New Haven: Yale University Press, 1948), excerpted material from pages 484–516. Reprinted by permission.

United States was prepared to withdraw bag and baggage from the entire sphere of Greater East Asia and the South Seas, "(which God forbid), we are bound eventually to come to a head-on clash with Japan." President Roosevelt replied, January 21, 1941, "I find myself in decided agreement with your conclusions"; and went on to say that "our strategy of self-defense must be a global strategy which takes account of every front and takes advantage of every opportunity to contribute to our total security."[3] In other words, in January 1941, President Roosevelt envisaged a head-on clash with Japan as a phase of assistance to Great Britain in a world of inseparable spheres of interest. This conclusion squared with the conviction he had expressed to Admiral Richardson on October 8, 1940: Japan will make a mistake and we will enter the war. . . .

President Roosevelt's Warning Note to Japan on August 17, 1941

On August 17, 1941, after his return from the Atlantic Conference, President Roosevelt called the Japanese Ambassador to the White House and told him point-blank, among other things:

. . . this Government now finds it necessary to say to the Government of Japan that if the Japanese Government takes any further steps in pursuance of a policy or program of military domination by force or threat of force of neighboring countries, the Government of the United States will be compelled to take immediately any and all steps which it may deem necessary toward safeguarding the legitimate rights and interests of the United States and American nationals and toward insuring the safety and security of the United States.

[3] Joseph C. Grew, *Ten Years in Japan* (Simon & Schuster, 1944), pp. 359 ff.

Such was the formula of the President's warning as recorded in the State Department's *Peace and War,* published in July, 1943 (p. 714).[4]

To the Japanese Ambassador, familiar with the language of diplomacy, the statement could have had only one meaning. Although the President did not even hint that he would appeal to Congress for a declaration of war if the Japanese Government failed to heed his warning, he did indicate that if that government took any further steps in the direction of dominating neighboring countries, by force or threat of force, the United States would do something besides send another diplomatic memorandum to Tokyo. . . .

In the memoranda made by Mr. Welles on the meetings at the Atlantic Conference it is patent that the notice given by President Roosevelt to the Japanese Ambassador on August 17, 1941, was intended to be in the nature of a war warning. It is true that in the final form given to the notice, two points brought up at

[4] I searched the files of the *New York Times* and the *New York Herald Tribune* from August 17 to August 31, 1941, for references to press releases or statements from the White House and the State Department bearing on the delivery of this warning notice to Ambassador Nomura and found no such reference. Later I had two independent searches made of these files by two scholars trained in historical research and neither of them found even a hint that this note had been delivered to the Japanese Ambassador. On December 16, 1946, I wrote to the State Department asking whether the department had issued any statement or press release on the note of August 17, 1941, and received a reply dated January 3, 1947, which did not constitute an answer. In a letter dated January 7, 1947, I directed this question to the State Department: "Did the Department of State issue on or after August 17, 1941, any press release or statement to the press notifying the public that the important memorandum of August 17, 1941, had been delivered to the Japanese Ambassador in Washington on that day?" In a letter dated January 21, 1947, the State Department said: "the records of the Department indicate that a press release was not issued on the subject to which you refer."

the Atlantic Conference had been eliminated or softened. Mr. Churchill's suggestion that the President inform Japan that he intended to seek authority from Congress to implement his notice was rejected. Also eliminated from the draft dated August 15, 1941, were the words: "notwithstanding the possibility that such further steps on its [Japan's] part may result in conflict between the two countries"; for these words were substituted a formula more veiled, but scarcely any less meaningful to Ambassador Nomura and the Government of Japan.

The Japanese Government's Proposal for a Pacific Conference Rejected

Numerous "leaks" in Washington, noncommittal releases from the Department of State, and rumors kept the American public in expectancy — and confusion. In fact, at one time, when it was openly said in newspaper circles that arrangements had been made for a meeting of President Roosevelt and Premier Konoye, this "rumor" was brushed aside humorously by the President's Secretary, Stephen Early, at the White House.[5]

Although, during the tortuous exchanges of notes on the proposed conference in the Pacific, the American public remained in the dark with regard to the nature of the various offers and counteroffers, documents made available since December 7, 1941, have partly disclosed the nature of the tactics employed by President Roosevelt and Secretary Hull in conducting those exchanges. . . .

The strategy pursued by the President and the Secretary of State during these conversations on the Japanese Premier's proposal for a peace conference in the Pacific was, in brief, as follows. The President and the Secretary expressed to Japan a willingness to consider favorably

[5] See above, p. 189.

the idea of a Pacific Conference, but insisted that the Premier should first agree upon certain principles in advance, with a view to assuring the success of the conference.

The Premier of Japan, on September 6, 1941, informed the American Ambassador in Tokyo that he subscribed fully to the four great principles of American policy laid down in Washington.[6] Then President Roosevelt and Secretary Hull declared that this was not enough, that agreements on more principles and formulas was necessary, that the replies of the Japanese Government were still unsatisfactory; but they refrained from saying in precise language just what it was they demanded in detail as fixed conditions for accepting the Japanese invitation to a conference in the Pacific. To meet their obvious distrust of Japanese authorities and especially the Japanese militarists, Premier Konoye assured them that he had authority for bringing with him to the conference high army and naval officers as evidence that his commitments would have the support of the Army and the Navy of Japan. Still the President and the Secretary continued adamant in their tactics of prolonging the conversations as if they were merely playing for time, "babying the Japanese along."

It may be said that President Roosevelt and Secretary Hull thus chose a course well within their discretion, and demonstrated wisdom in so doing. That militarists in the Japanese Government and outside had been engaged in barbaric practices in China for many years and were rattling the sabers in the autumn of 1941 was a matter of general knowledge in the United States. That the Roosevelt Administration had long been opposed to Japan's policies and measures was, at

[6] *Peace and War*, pp. 733 ff.

least, equally well known. Still, if keeping out of war in the Pacific was a serious issue for the United States, then the primary question for President Roosevelt and Secretary Hull was: Did the Japanese proposal offer an opportunity to effect a settlement in the Pacific and were the decisions they made in relation to it actually "looking" in the direction of peace? . . .

Aware that in negotiations with the Japanese Ambassador in Washington, President Roosevelt and Secretary Hull were insisting upon further explorations of the Japanese proposal and that more than a month had passed in these "exploratory" operations, Mr. Grew warned them against this procedure. He told them that if the United States expected or awaited "clear-cut commitments" which would satisfy the United States "both as to principle and as to concrete detail," the conversations would be drawn out indefinitely and unproductively "until the Konoye cabinet and its supporting elements desiring rapprochement with the United States will come to the conclusion that the outlook for an agreement is hopeless and that the United States Government is only playing for time."[7] In this case, the Ambassador continued, the Konoye Government would be discredited. "The logical outcome of this will be the downfall of the Konoye cabinet and the formation of a military dictatorship which will lack either the disposition or the temperament to avoid colliding head-on with the United States."

If Premier Konoye was sincere in his intentions why could he not give President Roosevelt and Secretary Hull clear-cut commitments as to details before the

[7] Did this mean that the Japanese would suspect that President Roosevelt's intention was "to baby them along," as Davis and Lindley represented his designs at the Atlantic Conference? *How War Came*, p. 10.

conference? To this central question Ambassador Grew gave serious attention and provided for the President and the Secretary an answer based on his knowledge of the critical situation in Tokyo. Mr. Grew knew that a "liberal" government in Japan, or indeed any government inclined to keep peace with the United States, was beset by the militarist and chauvinist press, always engaged in frightening and inflaming the Japanese public by warmongering. He knew also, what had recently been demonstrated many times, that the head and members of any such government were likely to be assassinated in cold blood by desperate agents of "patriotic" societies. He knew and so did Premier Konoye that Axis secret agents and Japanese enemies of peace with the United States were boring within the Konoye Government and watching with Argus eyes every message or communication sent from Tokyo to Washington. In other words, Premier Konoye could not be sure that any note he dispatched to Washington, no matter how guardedly, would escape the vigilance of his enemies on every side in Japan.

This situation Ambassador Grew went into at length in his report of September 29, 1941, to Secretary Hull and President Roosevelt. He had been in close and confidential communication with Premier Konoye. On the basis of very intimate knowledge, he informed them that the Japanese Government was ready to undertake commitments other than those set down in the communications which had already passed. He reported, if in cautious language as befitted a diplomat, that he had been told that "Prince Konoye is in a position in direct negotiations with President Roosevelt to offer him assurances which, because of their far-reaching character, will not fail to satisfy the

United States." Mr. Grew added that he could not determine the truth of this statement, but he said definitely that while the Japanese Government could not overtly renounce its relations with the Axis Powers, it "actually has shown a readiness to reduce Japan's alliance adherence to a dead letter by its indication of willingness to enter formally into negotiations with the United States."

Thereupon Mr. Grew presented the alternatives as he saw them from his point of vantage in Tokyo. The Japanese military machine and army could be discredited by wholesale military defeat. That was one alternative. On the other hand the United States could place a "reasonable amount of confidence" in

the professed sincerity of intention and good faith of Prince Konoye and his supporters to mold Japan's future policy upon the basic principles they are ready to accept and then to adopt measures which gradually but loyally implement those principles, with it understood that the United States will implement its own commitments *pari passu* with the steps which Japan takes.

This was the alternative which the American Ambassador commended to President Roosevelt and Secretary Hull as "an attempt to produce a regeneration of Japanese thought and outlook through constructive conciliation, along the lines of American efforts at present."

As to the alternatives, Mr. Grew closed his plea by inquiring "whether the better part of wisdom and of statesmanship is not to bring such efforts to a head before the force of their initial impetus is lost, leaving it impossible to overcome an opposition which the Ambassador thinks will mount inevitably and steadily in Japan." In Mr. Grew's opinion it was evidently a question of now or never, though he ended by paying deference to "the

much broader field of view of President Roosevelt and Secretary Hull" as compared with "the viewpoint of the American Embassy in Tokyo." . . .

Nevertheless, President Roosevelt and Secretary Hull rejected the advice of their Ambassador in Japan and prolonged the "explorations" until the Konoye Cabinet fell about two weeks later, October 16, 1941. Why? Records now available provide no answer. As far as the President was concerned, the question remains open, save for such inferences as may be drawn from collateral documents. Secretary Hull's answer is to be sought in many words spread over many pages, and, owing to the fact that he was the President's agent in the conduct of foreign affairs, his answer, by inference, may be treated as that of the Administration. When Secretary Hull's prolix and involved explanations as yet presented to the American public are all analyzed, compared, and tabulated, they amount to this: The Japanese had a long record of barbaric deeds; Prince Konoye was not much better, if any, than the bloodthirsty militarists; the promises and proposals of the Konoye Government were not to be trusted as offering any hope of peace to the "peace-loving nations of the world," as represented by the United States. . . .

In other words, the President and Secretary Hull regarded the Japanese proposal for a Pacific Conference as essentially dishonest, as if a kind of subterfuge to deceive the Government of the United States while Japan went on with aggression and conquest.

It is at present impossible to determine the parts played by President Roosevelt and Secretary Hull respectively in the final decision to reject the Konoye proposal, as it is in the case of their action on the memorandum of November 26, 1941. According to Premier Konoye's Memoirs

(CJC, Part 20, Exhibit 173), the President was at first enthusiastic about the idea of a conference in the Pacific but Secretary Hull was at the outset cool and at length resolute in pursuing the course which, as Ambassador Grew had warned him in effect, would end in failure and war.

Nor is it possible now to discover whether, if the Pacific conference had been held, Premier Konoye could have carried out his intentions as communicated to the President and Secretary Hull. It is easy, of course, to take passages from Premier Konoye's Memoirs, and other fragmentary documents at present available, for the purpose of making an argument for or against American acceptance of his proposal; but, as Ambassador Grew informed the President and Secretary Hull at the time, the alternative of war would remain open to the United States if the conference had not fulfilled expectations. The "solution" of this insoluble "problem," however, lies outside the purposes and limitations of my inquiry.

The Japanese Proposal of a Modus Vivendi Rejected in Favor of an Ultimative Notice

Though the Konoye Cabinet in Tokyo had been succeeded by what was regarded as a "strong" government headed by General Hideki Tojo, supposed to be an irreconcilable militarist, the Japanese did not break off conversations "looking to the maintenance of peace in the Pacific." On the contrary, the Japanese Government early in November dispatched to Ambassador Nomura two proposals for new discussions to be taken up with President Roosevelt and Secretary Hull and sent a special agent, Saburo Kurusu, to assist the Ambassador in further explorations. The first of these proposals, called proposal "A," was plainly a document for bargaining; the second, proposal "B," was more conciliatory and had the signs of being the last offer the Japanese Government might make to the United States — "a last effort to prevent something happening." Was this move on the part of Japan just another evidence of what Secretary Hull called Japanese trickery, a desire to prolong negotiations and to deceive the Government of the United States?

On their face the two proposals, as finally presented to the State Department, might have been so regarded by Secretary Hull. But as a matter of fact, having previously broken the Japanese code, American Navy and Army Intelligence had intercepted, translated, and made available to the Administration, before either of the projects had been laid before Secretary Hull, the substance of the two documents as sent in code from Tokyo to Ambassador Nomura. It had done more. It had intercepted accompanying messages from Tokyo to the Ambassador which indicated, in the first place, that the Tojo Cabinet was anxious to reach some kind of settlement with the United States; and, in the next place, that the second proposal was, to use the language of the Japanese dispatch containing it, "advanced with the idea of making a last effort to prevent something from happening." If the opinion often expressed by Secretary Hull to the effect that the Japanese were chronic liars be accepted as correct, still it is hardly to be presumed that the Japanese Government was lying to its Ambassador when, in secret messages intended for his eyes alone, it informed him that a settlement was urgently desired in Tokyo and that proposal "B" was to be offered in a last effort to prevent something from happening — that is, doubtless, an open break and war.[8]

[8] CJC, Part 12, Exhibit 1, for the two proposals,

In short, Secretary Hull knew in advance, on November 4, 1941, that the Japanese proposals were coming to him, that the Tokyo Government had expressed to Ambassador Nomura anxiety to reach some settlement with the United States, that it had fixed November 25 as a deadline, that failure to achieve a settlement or truce meant drastic action, if not war, on the part of the Japanese Government. On November 1, Secretary Hull had asked the Army and Navy whether they were ready to give support to new warnings to Japan, and expressed the opinion that there was no use to issue any additional warnings "if we can't back them up."[9] On November 5, General Marshall and Admiral Stark addressed to President Roosevelt a memorandum in which they strongly objected to military action against Japan at the moment and urged the postponement of hostilities in order to allow the Army and Navy as much time as possible to effect better preparations for war.[10] It was in this state of affairs that Secretary Hull undertook to deal with Ambassador Nomura when

he presented a sketch of proposal "A," November 7, 1941. . . .

When President Roosevelt and Secretary Hull were called upon to make decisions with regard to the Japanese program for a kind of modus vivendi looking to a general settlement in the Pacific, they confronted a fateful choice and they knew it. From secret Japanese messages intercepted by the Army and Navy Intelligence, they had learned that this proposal was the final offering from the Japanese Government. They confronted the urgent appeal from General Marshall and Admiral Stark to postpone hostilities with Japan on the ground that the Army and Navy were not ready for war. Should at least a truce of some form be attempted if only to give the United States more time to prepare for war? The idea of a truce had been taken up by the President with Secretary Stimson as early as November 6, two days after the secret Japanese message on the negotiations had been intercepted.[11] And Mr. Stimson had strongly objected to the idea.[12]

Despite Secretary Stimson's objections, however, the President apparently decided that a truce or modus vivendi might and should be attempted; for he sent an undated note to Secretary Hull, giving his suggestions for the terms of such a temporary or preliminary adjustment with Japan. The President's note contained the following points:

6 Months

1. United States to resume economic relations — some oil and rice now — more later.

2. Japan to send no more troops to Indo-China or Manchurian border or any place South (Dutch, Brit. or Siam).

3. Japan to agree not to invoke tripartite pact even if the U.S. gets into European war.

4. U.S. to introduce Japs to Chinese to

pp. 94–97; for various relevant Japanese messages, intercepted and translated by American Intelligence, pp. 90 ff.

[9] At a meeting of the Joint Board of the Army and Navy, November 3, 1941, General Marshall and Admiral Stark present, among others, Captain R. E. Schuirmann, liaison officer between the Office of Naval Operations and the State Department, reported on actions at the State Department meeting on November 1. Captain Schuirmann "pointed out that on August 17, following the President's return from the meeting at sea with Mr. Churchill, the President had issued an ultimatum to Japan that it would be necessary for the United States to take action in case of further Japanese aggression. . . . Mr. Hull was of the opinion that there was no use to issue any additional warnings to Japan if we can't back them up, and he desired to know if the military authorities would be prepared to support further warnings by the State Department." CJC, Part 14, p. 1063. The Japanese deadline was later moved to November 29. CJC, Part 20, p. 165.

[10] CJC, Part 12, Exhibit 1; Part 14, Exhibits 16, 18.

[11] See above, pp. 507 ff.

[12] Stimson, Diary, for November 6, 1941.

talk things over but U.S. to take no part in their conversation. . . .

It was amid complicated circumstances that Secretary Hull worked at the problem raised by the Japanese proposal for a truce or modus vivendi. He knew from intercepts of secret Japanese messages that this was regarded in Tokyo as the "last effort" on the part of the Japanese Government. Should he make a blunt reply or resort to supreme diplomatic ingenuity in an attempt to keep conversations going in the hope of peace in the Pacific or at least postponing war for a time until the American Army and Navy were better equipped to fight it? He knew that on August 17, 1941, President Roosevelt had served a warning notice on Tokyo to the effect that in case of any further Japanese encroachments on their neighbors, the United States would take steps that meant war. He knew that during all the explorations since August, the position then taken had been firmly maintained, that the war plans for cooperation with Great Britain, the Netherlands, and Australia were all predicated upon joint action against Japan if she moved southward beyond definite boundary lines. Secretary Hull was well aware that General Marshall and Admiral Stark had been and were pressing for more time in which to prepare the Army and Navy for war. Was it not for him a matter of supreme statesmanship to prevent, if humanly possible, a two-front war for the United States — a war in the Pacific as well as the "shooting war" in the Atlantic?

As far as the documentary record goes, Secretary Hull for a few days at least considered a modus vivendi with Japan desirable and feasible. From November 22 to November 26, the Secretary, in consultation with the President and the highest military authorities, worked over proposals and plans for some kind of adjust-

ment with Japan on the basis of the Japanese note of November 20.[13] In this connection the project was discussed with representatives of Great Britain, Australia, the Netherlands, and China. The principles of the final draft were approved by Secretary Stimson, who declared that it adequately safeguarded "American interests."

Alarmed lest the Government of the United States make something like a truce or temporary standstill with Japan, with a view to further negotiation actually looking to the maintenance of peace in the Pacific, Chinese diplomatic and special agents, supported by powerful American interests, made a storm over the proposed modus vivendi with Japan. In this operation, they were ably led by the Chinese Ambassador, Dr. Hu Shih, a liberal, wise in the ways of the West and the East, once well marked by the dread police of the Chiang Kai-shek Government, now serving it in the United States where "liberalism" was an asset. From day to day, hour to hour, the Chinese and their agents bombarded Secretary Hull so heavily with protests against any truce with Japan that the situation in Washington became almost hysterical.

This state of affairs was later described by Secretary Hull himself. The Secretary, in a subsequent statement relative to the pressures then brought to bear on him by the Chinese, declared that Chiang Kai-shek "has sent numerous hysterical cable messages to different cabinet officers and high officials in the Government other than the State Department, and sometimes even ignoring the President, intruding into a delicate and serious situation with no real idea of what the facts are."

[13] Various drafts of the proposed modus vivendi with Japan are to be found in *ibid.* (CJC), along with other relevant documents. For a digest of Mr. Hull's account, see CJC, *Report*, pp. 33 ff.

Secretary Hull further said that "Chiang Kai-shek had his brother-in-law, located here in Washington, disseminate damaging reports at times to the press and others, apparently with no particular purpose in mind." Besieged by Chinese agents in London, Prime Minister Churchill, instead of supporting his Ambassador in Washington, Lord Halifax, who was eager for a truce in the Pacific, intervened by sending a confusing message as if trying to support the Chinese side of the dispute with the Government of the United States.

Disturbed by the vacillations introduced by Mr. Churchill's intrusion into American affairs, Secretary Hull exclaimed that

it would have been better if, when Churchill received Chiang Kai-shek's loud protest about our negotiations here with Japan, instead of passing the protest on to us without objection on his part, thereby qualifying and virtually killing what we knew were the individual views of the British Government toward these negotiations, he had sent a strong cable back to Chiang Kai-shek telling him to brace up and fight with the same zeal as the Japanese and the Germans are displaying instead of weakening and telling the Chinese people that all of the friendly countries were now striving primarily to protect themselves and to force an agreement between China and Japan. Every Chinese should understand from such a procedure that the best possible course was being pursued and that this calls for resolute fighting until the undertaking is consummated by peace negotiations which Japan in due course would be obliged to enter into with China.[14]

In other words, while the negotiations over the Japanese proposal for a modus vivendi were proceeding, Secretary Hull was disgusted with the operations of Chinese agents. He was convinced that the

[14] CJC, Part 14, pp. 1194 ff.

tentatives of the proposal should be explored and efforts be made to reach some kind of basis for further explorations in the direction of a settlement in the Far East. He was likewise convinced that in the proceedings along this line the real interests of China could be protected by the United States, indeed advanced, until, at least, the willingness of Japan to come to decent terms could be probed to the bottom. So at least, it seems.

But for reasons which are nowhere explicit, despite the thousands of words on the subject that appear in the Pearl Harbor documents and testimony, Secretary Hull, after consulting President Roosevelt, suddenly and completely abandoned the project and on November 26, 1941, handed the Japanese Ambassador and Mr. Kurusu the historic memorandum which the Japanese Government treated as an ultimatum.[15] When the Japanese representatives in Washington read the document, Mr. Kurusu assured the Secretary that the Japanese Government, after examining it, would be likely to throw up its hands. When, the next morning, Secretary Stimson asked Secretary Hull what had been done about the modus vivendi project, the Secretary replied that "he had broken the whole matter off." He then added: "I have washed my hands of it and it is now in the hands of you and Knox — the Army and the Navy." . . .[16]

[15] For the nature and significance of this memorandum, see above, Chap. IX; and for the upshot of the decision to send it, see below, pp. 555 ff.
[16] Alden Hatch, who claims to have inside information from prominent persons close to President Roosevelt at the time, seems to ascribe this momentous decision mainly to Secretary Hull, for he says: "Roosevelt was uncertain if he had done the right thing in allowing Hull to present his ten-point program to Japan on November 26. Though it offered them great economic concessions, and the access to the goods of the Indies that they desired, it called on them to desist in China. He feared they would never do that." *Franklin D. Roosevelt: An Informal Biography,* p. 289.

Basil Rauch: ROOSEVELT AND JAPAN: AN INTERNATIONAL POLICY

Introduction

DURING the decade 1933–1942, world events and President Franklin D. Roosevelt led the American people and their government to adopt collective security as the foreign policy of the United States. The late Dr. Charles A. Beard is the only historian who has written on the process by which the nation abandoned isolationism and turned to internationalism. His two books, *American Foreign Policy in the Making: 1932–1940: A Study in Responsibilities,* and *President Roosevelt and the Coming of the War: 1941: A Study in Appearances and Realities,* frankly aim to destroy the faith of Americans in the honesty of President Roosevelt in planning the new foreign policy.

These books propose a revisionist interpretation of the causes of American entry into the Second World War. After the First World War, revisionist historians won over the American public to their view that the United States had entered that war not because Germany committed aggression against it, but because American bankers and munitions manufacturers plotted entry for their own profit. The thesis provided justification for the return to isolationism. Beard's purpose was to create a similar disillusionment regarding the reasons for American entry into the recent war, and a similar revulsion against the foreign policy of internationalism.

The villain in Beard's plot is not an economic group with a vested interest in war, but the President of the United States acting for motives which are not defined. The picture of President Roosevelt engaged in a colossal and profoundly immoral plot to deceive the American people into participating in the war unnecessarily and contrary to their interests might be thought so overdrawn as to be unconvincing. But Beard relies upon the effects of the twelve and more years of widely publicized hatred of Roosevelt by a minority of the public and the majority of the press to make the familiarity of his characterization overcome its implausibility.

An indication of Beard's desire to capitalize on anti-Roosevelt feeling is that in his two books he almost completely ignores the part Secretary of State Hull played in the making of administration foreign policy. Hull's work was certainly second in importance only to that of the President himself, and in details it was more revealing than Roosevelt's. But, because Hull was generally regarded as an honest and safe leader, his presence on Beard's stage as Roosevelt's partner would have been an inartistic contradiction of Beard's image of Roosevelt pursuing a sinister plot.

This is only one of the many artful exclusions Beard practices. More important is his exclusion of any data on the objective course of world events which might suggest that the United States, confronted by rising Axis power, did actually face

From *Roosevelt: From Munich to Pearl Harbor,* copyright 1950 by Basil Rauch, Creative Age Press — Farrar, Straus and Young, Inc., publishers.

danger to its own security. In Beard's books, not policies of Hitler or Japan but the policies of Roosevelt created first the danger and then the fact of United States participation in the Second World War. In the early pages of *American Foreign Policy in the Making*, Beard shows admirable, perhaps even excessive, respect for the complexities of problems of historical causation, but only in order to justify his own failure to assess the part of the aggressor nations in causing the Second World War. Thereafter Beard proceeds in the remainder of that book and throughout his second one to make a masterpiece of oversimplification in order to lay responsibility for war upon Roosevelt.

Besides excluding material essential for the understanding of Roosevelt's foreign policy, Beard violently distorts the material he does use. His principal distortions are two: that internationalists, led by Roosevelt during the thirties, wanted the United States to go to war; and that Roosevelt practiced deception on the American people regarding the nature and aims of his foreign policy.

The first of these distortions depends upon a perverse definition of internationalism. Beard lifts his definition from the lexicon of isolationism and uses it in both his books as axiomatic truth. His complete definition follows:

Here and in the following pages the term *internationalism* is used as meaning: World peace is desirable and possible; it is indivisible and can be secured for the United States only by entering into a positive connection with a league, or association, of nations, empowered to make pacific adjustments of international conflicts and to impose peace, by effective sanctions or by force, on aggressors or peace breakers; the United States cannot maintain neutrality in case of any major war among European and Asiatic powers.

This definition is fair enough up to the word "only," which, strengthened as it is by the word "positive," falsifies the program of American internationalists, especially of the time when President Roosevelt came to office, as if the *ultimate* step by the United States in the direction of collective security, that is, "a positive connection with a league, or association, of nations," was the "only" and therefore the *first* step they advocated. The Roosevelt administration never advocated United States entry into the League of Nations. It did advocate parallel action with the League in particular cases, after the United States should have first decided independently in each case that the action of the League corresponded to the interests and policy of the United States. Whether independent and parallel action with the League of Nations may be termed a "positive connection with a league" is debatable, but it is also beside the point.

The heart of the argument was that isolationists during the period between the two World Wars asserted the impossibility of the United States taking part in collective action against an aggressor without forming "entangling alliances" and making "prior commitments" which would destroy the sovereignty of the United States and permit other nations to determine its policy and even plunge it into war against its will. This was the chief argument against joining the League after the First World War. Henry L. Stimson, President Hoover's Secretary of State, President Roosevelt, and Secretary Hull were, nonetheless, internatiounalists even though they conceded to the power of this argument. Their statesmanship consisted in devising techniques which would permit the United States to take part in international action for collective security without forming entangling alliances or making prior commitments. One such was the technique of "parallel action"; another was "consultation," whereby the United States promised to consult with other nations when aggression occurred, but reserved the right to judge for itself in each case whether it should take action against the aggressor; a third was a discriminatory arms embargo against aggressors; a fourth was Lend Lease; a fifth was the "veto power" of the United States in the Security Council of the United Nations, which not only avoids prior commitment by the United States to take action in any particular case, but enables the United States to prevent the Security Council itself from taking action.

The development of such techniques is of supreme importance in the history of collective security as an American policy. It is sometimes argued that these techniques compromised the policy of collective security to the point of obliteration. In this view, the effective policy of the United States under Roosevelt shifted not from isolation to collective security but from isolation to participation in world politics to protect the United States and increase its power at the expense of other powers. Whether this is indeed a fair statement of the "inner meaning" of Roosevelt's policy will be discussed here after. In either case, Roosevelt's method was cooperation with some powers against others; the method was supported by internationalists and the development certainly marked a change in United States foreign policy. Whatever the "inner meaning" of this development, isolationists denied that national sovereignty could be preserved by any method except abstinence from cooperation with other governments; they asserted that the ob-

ject of the new policy was not peace but war, and Beard perpetuates their distortions as "truths of history."

The new techniques enabled Roosevelt and other leaders to go before the country and plead for collective security, and at the same time promise in good faith that they did not contemplate entangling alliances or prior commitments and that they had as their greatest purpose avoidance of United States participation in war. Throughout his two books, Beard calls such promises "retreats" from the policy of collective security or "denials" of that policy and examples of how Roosevelt "misled" the people. Evidently parallel action, consultation, and a discriminatory arms embargo do not constitute for Beard a "positive connection with a league." Positive or not, these techniques constituted the program of American internationalism during the thirties, and Beard's definition of that word evades, as isolationists generally evaded, that fact, in order to make the false charge that internationalism did involve entangling alliances and prior commitments — and war.

Collective security, the isolationists charged, would involve the United States in war. It would be a most evil war because entangling alliances and prior commitments would make it an "offensive" war, one that was "none of our business," fought by the United States "against our will," "to pull other people's chestnuts out of the fire." The President was accused of advocating internationalism *because* it would involve the United States in war. Beard arranges his definition of internationalism to lead his readers into acceptance of the charge as truth. The central argument of internationalists, that collective security is precisely the only means whereby the United States can *avoid* war, he distorts into a charge that they believe in using force, not solely as a last recourse *after* peaceful moral, diplomatic, economic, and political sanctions have failed to halt an aggressor, but at the outset, as an *alternative* to other sanctions. The word "or" in Beard's definition ". . . impose peace, by effective sanctions or by force, . . ." mashes into one lump the series of measures, carefully graded from less to more coercive, with which internationalists believe an aggressor should be faced — those measures to be applied successively, with the hope and reasonable expectation that the threat of stronger measures would, at a stage short of war, stop the aggressor. No reasonable observer is likely to argue that, if all the allied and associated powers that ultimately combined to win the First and Second World Wars had combined before those wars began and faced Germany and its allies with the certainty of their collective action, those wars would have occurred.

A fair definition of internationalism must specify that the policy involves a series of collective measures, graded from less to more coercive, by a group of nations having a large share of world power, and the reasoned conviction of internationalists that the threat of these measures will stop aggression before the last one, force, is reached. Thus the central, simple fact may be understood: internationalists support collective measures against aggression as the best means of securing world peace.

Beard's other chief distortion — that Roosevelt practiced deception on the American people regarding the nature and aims of his foreign policy — depends upon his distorted definition of internationalism. Beard proves in great detail that Roosevelt repeatedly assured the American people that his policy was to avoid entangling alliances, prior commitments, and war. He finds deception in these assurances because an internationalist policy, in Beard's view, could not avoid entangling alliances, prior commitments, and war.

His thesis is maintained by butchering the record and throwing out its most vital parts. Roosevelt, from his first to his last days in office, not only repeatedly assured the American people that his policy was to avoid entangling alliances, prior commitments and war, but he devised and repeatedly urged upon the public and Congress techniques of collective security which, while avoiding entangling alliances and prior commitments, he as an internationalist was convinced were the best means of preventing United States involvement in war.

A shift that occurred in January, 1939, was not a shift in policy but in emphasis. Before his Annual Message of that year, President Roosevelt placed primary emphasis on the achievement of domestic reforms and only secondary emphasis on the achievement of collective security as the foreign policy of the United States. From 1933 to November, 1939, every attempt to achieve the latter outside the Western Hemisphere was defeated by Congress. The Munich crisis of September, 1938, and Roosevelt's conviction that the "settlement" made war certain, motivated a shift. In his Message of January, 1939, Roosevelt announced that the order or emphasis was reversed: thenceforth the administration would seek no new domestic reforms but would place the achievement of collective security first on its program.

A change in administration policy did occur in the field of economic, as opposed to political, foreign policy. From 1933 to about 1935 the Roosevelt administration was led by the domestic economic crisis to pursue foreign policies of economic nationalism designed to support such measures as the National Industrial Recovery Act and the Agricultural Adjustment Act. These economic foreign policies contradicted and weakened the first efforts at collective security in political foreign relations. Secretary Hull opposed them, but the President assured him they were temporary expedients, and Hull's patience and persistence were rewarded when the President kept his promise, reversed himself, and, between 1934 and 1936, installed the entire Hull program of economic internationalism. Both Hull and Roosevelt never lost sight of the truth that economic internationalism is a necessary and solid foundation for political internationalism and, therefore, world peace.

The new American economic policy led the peaceful nations of the world to liquidate economic rivalries among themselves and form ties of great political and military as well as economic significance in opposition to the Axis nations. In perspective, the Roosevelt administration's internationalist economic policy may be called the taproot of the political and military united front which the peaceful nations organized too late to prevent the Second World War but in time to win it and make their victory a victory for collective security and the United Nations.

Beard, whose most valuable contribution to the understanding of American history was his exploration of the influence of economics on politics, might be expected to admit that a definition of internationalism which neglects economic policy is inadequate. His own writings suggest that certain nationalist economic doctrines influenced his political isola-

tionism and make his elimination of the economic category from his presentation of internationalism the more astonishing.

The policy of internationalism also includes much that lies beyond the economic and political spheres. It involves attitudes of respect towards foreign peoples and cultures and their governments, no matter how weak they may be in material power. It is the opposite of provincialism, chauvinism, and imperialism. One needs only to think of the attitudes and policies of Hitler, whom no one will accuse of being an internationalist, to understand what internationalism is by its opposites. When American isolationists adopted the slogan "America First" as the name of their directing committee, they implied that internationalists do not place the interests of their own country first, which is not true, but isolationists' actual policy and propaganda was "America First and Last — Other Nations and Peoples Nowhere," and this did distinguish them from internationalists.

An internationalist welcomes the diversities and contributions of peoples other than his own group as enrichments of his thinking and living. He is free of those attitudes of inferiority and insecurity which lead an isolationist to struggle to exclude from his thinking and living influences tainted by "foreignness" as threats to his identity. Fear, suspicion, hatred, and contempt of foreign peoples and cultures were remarkably absent among the leaders of the Roosevelt administration and the President set a tone thoroughly internationalist in spirit. By way of contrast, one may recall the contemptuous epithets President Theodore Roosevelt commonly hurled at foreigners, especially those not of "Teutonic" race. Innumerable trivial and important activities of the Franklin D. Roosevelt administration illustrated the spiritual and material values of internationalism in spheres ramified beyond, yet organically related to, internationalist economic and political programs.

While it will be impossible in this book to pursue further these broadest aspects of Rooseveltian internationalism, it will be useful to notice two of its corollaries as amplifications of the meaning of internationalism. The first is that internationalism is incompatible with imperialism. Historical reason exists for the common identification of the two. During the McKinley-Theodore Roosevelt era, United States policy was frankly imperialist, and anti-imperialists were reasonably designated "isolationists" because their argument was that "we should stop meddling in foreign countries and come home and mind our own business." Anti-imperialists came to power with Woodrow Wilson and again with Franklin D. Roosevelt, but they were not content merely to liquidate imperialist positions established by McKinley and Theodore Roosevelt and to retire into isolation. They worked for foreign policies of international cooperation that called for even more "meddling" even farther "away from home" than did imperialism. Their conversion of those imperialist positions which they did not liquidate into supports for policies of international cooperation made the application of correct labels quite difficult. Thus the naval policies of the two Roosevelts seemed identical because they both "loved the Navy," both built "big" navies, and they both used these spectacular instruments with considerable freedom to support their foreign policies. But a surgeon's knife can be used either to cure or to kill. The two Roosevelts used the United States Navy for opposite purposes — the one imperialist and the other internationalist.

When internationalists controlled an administration the imperialists used the arguments of, and were called, isolationists. In short, isolationism is the policy of the "outs" and no administration in this century has actually practiced it. The Harding-Coolidge administrations, caught between the unpopularity of imperialism and the temporary defeat of internationalism, came closest, but with a margin in favor of imperialism, especially of the more cryptic economic varieties.

The public rejection, first of imperialism and then of isolationism, has made the two words semantically poisonous for political use. Those isolationists of the thirties who, unlike pacifists and doctrinaires, were aware of the impossibility of isolation and wished for an imperialist program found it necessary to devise phrases with which they could smuggle their cause into the good graces of unwary internationalists. They spoke of the necessity of the United States assuming its rightful international responsibilities.

In theoretical debate both imperialism and internationalism are opposites of isolation, and this enables the unpopular cause of imperialism to masquerade as internationalism. These two are, in fact, also opposites of each other, and in the practical conduct of the United States government's foreign relations they are the only alternatives. The seemingly objective test of whether an administration retains or acquires territorial positions is useless because such positions may be used, as were the American bases acquired from Britain in 1940, for thoroughly anti-imperialist purposes and to support the policy of internationalism. The best available test of whether an administration is imperialist or internationalist is found in its attitudes towards foreign peoples and their governments, because these attitudes determine whether the use that is made of power wielded outside the national boundaries will be favorable or unfavorable to foreign rights and interests. The Roosevelt administration illustrated the incompatibility of internationalism and imperialism and effectively installed the former as the policy of the United States.

The other corollary of Rooseveltian internationalism is that it placed the administration in the main stream of the American tradition of democratic idealism. This won support for the policy from many at home who were still dubious of political and economic internationalism, as well as devotion from the rank and file of peoples throughout the world. It was one of several respects in which Roosevelt revived creative democratic, as opposed to inert conservative, forces in American civilization.

Inert conservative forces provided the chief strength of isolationism during the Roosevelt era. To these were annexed, on one side, extreme nationalist elements and those sympathetic to the Axis, and on the other those who raised pacifism to the status of an absolute principle destructive of all other principles of law, order, and self-defense. But these two wings did not include those nationalists who understood that internationalism was the best guaranty of national interest or those pacifists who understood that collective security was the best guaranty of peace, and they were correspondingly weak. The great mass of isolationists was simply conservative, and the main body of isolationist propaganda was designed to fortify the conservative temper. Like most conservative political doctrines, isolationism appealed for loyalty to a past that never existed.

The United States has never been isolated. Throughout its history it has played an active part in international economic,

cultural, and political life. The Founding Fathers, whose example the isolationists so ardently and mistakenly invoked, organized in 1778 the French Alliance containing a grand array of economic, political, and military prior commitments and entanglements of decisive value in securing the independence of the United States. This was a permanent alliance. Isolationists of the nineteen-thirties daily libeled President George Washington as the author, in his Farewell Address, of the dictum "no entangling alliances." This was actually Thomas Jefferson's phrase. Washington could not completely repudiate the instrument which had saved his victory as Commander-in-Chief of the Continental Army. In his Farewell Address he wisely condemned *permanent* alliances because the existing government of the French Revolution was using the American Alliance to make the United States a vassal of France in its war against Great Britain. Washington at the same time specifically approved *temporary* alliances for the United States. Jefferson, the chief architect of theoretical isolationism, was also readiest to abandon it when need arose, as when he gave orders to Monroe to make an alliance with Britain if Napoleon persisted in his design to occupy Louisiana and, when Monroe was President, advised acceptance of Canning's 1823 proposal for an Anglo-American entente against the Holy Alliance.

It happened that no full-fledged alliance was ever again signed by the United States after the French Alliance was terminated in 1800. President Monroe and Secretary of State John Quincy Adams formulated the unilateral Monroe Doctrine, contrary to Jefferson's advice, because they understood that Britain would defend the independence of the Western Hemisphere against the Continental powers out of self-interest, without a pledge to the United States, and they wanted to be free to combat British ambitions within the Hemisphere and make annexations of territory against which Canning demanded a pact of mutual self-denial.

But the Clayton-Bulwer Treaty of 1850, providing joint Anglo-American guaranties regarding an isthmian canal, certainly constituted a prior commitment by the United States and not only entangled it in British designs but also entangled Britain in American affairs so deeply that the Taylor administration was accused of signing away the Monroe Doctrine. The Monroe Doctrine was, of course, a prior commitment to support some twenty foreign nations against aggression, but it enjoyed exemption from the rules of isolationism. The United States from time to time made similar commitments regarding territory outside the Western Hemisphere, such as the Hawaiian and Samoan Islands, and these also were ignored in public professions of isolationist purity.

At the turn of the century, commitments to the Open Door in China and Morocco entangled the United States in the power politics of Asia and Europe. The "unwritten alliance" between the United States and Britain after 1896 developed ties stronger, if anything, than those ordinarily created by paper alliances. During the nineteen-twenties, Republican administrations, while claiming credit among isolationists for violating their 1920 campaign pledge to join, if not the League of Nations, "an association of nations," entered into multilateral engagements in the Washington Treaties regarding the Open Door in China, the territorial status of Asia, and the size of the United States Navy. In the Kellogg-Briand Pact the United States made a prior commitment to the powers not to use offensively its highest instrument of national policy: war.

Beyond these and other fixed international political engagements, the United States throughout the course of its history continually and, following the formulations of Jefferson, with entire deliberation, played an active part in support of that *bête noire* of isolationists, the balance of power, first of Europe, then also of Asia, and finally on a world scale. Jefferson preached isolation but practiced involvement. It was only by an extraordinarily skillful manipulation of the weight of the United States in the scales of European power politics that such master diplomatists as Benjamin Franklin, John Jay, Thomas Jefferson, and John Quincy Adams secured the independence and expanded the territory and power of the United States. They promised friendship for, or threatened enmity against, the shifting sides in the European balance and wrung concessions to the United States in return for promises and threats. No other technique could, in the face of predatory empires, secure the growth of the United States from a weak to a great power. The rivalries of those empires opened the road to American success, but American diplomacy did not wait passively for chances to make gains: it intervened aggressively to widen divisions among them, resorting even to war in 1775, 1798, 1803, 1812, 1846, 1898, and 1917.

In the face of this history of American foreign commitments, diplomacy and wars, isolationists appealed to the authority of the past to consecrate a policy of nonparticipation in international affairs. They failed to understand the value to the United States of its commercial, political, and cultural ties with the world, and their dependence on the continued existence of civilizations abroad with which the United States could maintain such ties. Isolationists ordinarily ignored the very existence of those ties; they were the most embarrassing of all the contradictions of the isolationist image of an arcadian, isolated, American past. Fear of the present and nostalgia for a fantasy of the past were the sources of isolationists' opposition to Rooseveltian internationalism.

Opposition to war was a more praiseworthy sentiment, and it was the chief public argument for isolation in foreign policy during the nineteen-thirties. So the debate revolved around the charge that the United States was more likely to become involved in war if it participated in measures of collective security. Beard has Roosevelt's advocacy of collective security and United States participation in the Second World War as his chief facts in evidence that the isolationists were right. It is the thesis of this book that his fallacy is the ancient one, *post hoc ergo propter hoc*, and that he has maintained it by distorting and excising the record. . . .

Grew Proposes "Constructive Conciliation"

The most important comment, during the whole period, on the Roosevelt-Hull conduct of negotiations with Japan was made on September 29 by Ambassador Grew in a report to Secretary Hull. This report raised the question whether there was not a vista open to the Roosevelt administration located somewhere between the road of appeasement and the road of refusal to appease which might end in war. . . .

In conclusion Grew gave his opinion that the United States would not reach its objective by insisting in preliminary conversations that Japan provide "the

sort of clear-cut, specific commitments which appear in any final, formal convention or treaty." Confidence must be placed in the good faith of Konoye and his supporters

to mould Japan's future policy upon the basic principles they are ready to accept and then to adopt measures which gradually but loyally implement those principles, with it understood that the United States will implement its own commitments *pari passu* with the steps Japan takes. . . .

This was what Grew meant by "constructive conciliation," and it was, he asserted, the only alternative to wholesale military defeat of Japan. The Ambassador ended by deferring to "the much broader field of view of President Roosevelt and Secretary Hull," and he expressed "full awareness" that his own approach was "limited to the viewpoint of the American Embassy in Japan."[1]

Secretary Hull makes no reference in his *Memoirs* to this significant report. It must engage the attention of anyone attempting to judge the Roosevelt-Hull policy. In the absence of comment by Hull, it may nevertheless be ventured to estimate his and Roosevelt's view of Grew's proposal on the basis of their known actions and general views. Hull in close contact with Roosevelt prepared a comprehensive statement to the Japanese government which he handed to Nomura on October 2. It amounted to an answer to Grew.[2]

Grew's proposal for "constructive conciliation" was vitiated by a basic error of fact. Roosevelt and Hull did not refuse to hold the meeting with Konoye because,

[1] *Foreign Relations: Japan,* II, 645–50. Also in Grew, *Ten Years in Japan,* 436–42.

[2] *Memoirs of Cordell Hull,* II, 1033. *Foreign Relations: Japan,* II, 656–61.

as Grew stated in his report, the Japanese failed to provide beforehand "the sort of clear-cut, specific commitments which appear in any final, formal convention or treaty," or because "moderates" in the Japanese government could not "define its future assurances and commitments more specifically than hitherto stated" for fear of pro-German officials. The Japanese government in its communications of September 6 and 22 had satisfied Roosevelt's and Hull's request for preliminary statements of its attitudes and purposes. Roosevelt and Hull refused to hold the meeting with Konoye for a quite different reason, namely, that *the Japanese proposals were unacceptable as a basis for agreement*. They meant nothing else than United States appeasement of Japan, which Grew himself had ruled out as a possible policy for the United States. In fact, they meant more than appeasement; they required United States cooperation with Japan in aggression.

Grew in his report emphasized Japan's agreement to American general principles for peace in the Pacific. He ignored the fact that the practical measures Japan proposed transformed those principles into their opposites. Grew asked Roosevelt and Hull to have faith that the Japanese government would adopt measures which would "gradually but loyally" implement those principles. But Konoye's first step in implementing them was to destroy them and ask the United States to help install opposite principles. If Roosevelt had met Konoye on the basis of the Japanese proposals, he himself would have been guilty of bad faith had he then refused to sign an agreement with Konoye to implement United States cooperation with Japan in aggression. . . .

The Last Chance?

The coming to power of Tojo ended

talk of a meeting between Roosevelt and the Japanese Premier. The administration in its efforts to maintain the secrecy of the negotiations, efforts insisted upon by the Japanese who feared the effects of publicity in rousing the militarists,[3] had publicly denied that Prince Konoye had "invited" Roosevelt to a Pacific conference. It was true that the stage of issuing an invitation was never reached. Beard treats the administration's uncommunicativeness as part of its plot to deceive the public by maintaing false "appearances."[4] In his exposition of the "realities" of the affair, Beard declares that Roosevelt and Hull not only pursued the "usual policy" of secrecy, but employed "dilatory" methods. Ambassador Grew's arguments in favor of "constructive conciliation" are Beard's chief evidence in support of his implication that Roosevelt and Hull wanted no reasonable settlement with Japan. But it is noteworthy that after carefully implanting in his reader's mind suspicion that Roosevelt and Hull deliberately rejected a reasonable opportunity for a settlement with Japan, Beard disclaims responsibility for arousing such suspicion by remarking that sufficient documents are not available for judgment. He admits that it is possible to find bases for argument *for,* as well as against Roosevelt's refusal to meet Konoye. Beard excuses his own failure to use the documents that are available because the " 'solution' of this insoluble 'problem' " lay outside the "purposes and limitations" of his book. After calling the Roosevelt-Konoye affair "momentous in the history of American relations with Japan," Beard's evasion of the problem, which would seem to be no more insoluble and is far more adequately documented than

[3] *Ibid.,* 1024.

[4] Beard, *Roosevelt,* 189–92.

most of the problems he claims to solve, is disappointing.[5]

Perhaps Beard had been discouraged by the statement in the Minority Report of the Pearl Harbor Joint Committee, that to go into the issue of the wisdom of the Roosevelt administration in its conduct of relations with Japan,

would involve the committee in the complexities of history extending back more than 50 years and in matters of opinion which cannot be settled by reference to anything as positive and definite as the Constitution, laws, and established administrative practices of the United States government.[6]

Besides, the question was excluded by the terms of the Committee's instructions. But the Committee did not fail to develop information on the subject in order to "understand the questions involved."

Morgenstern, more bold than Beard, examined evidence found by the Committee and other documents, and came to very clear conclusions. "Diplomacy," he writes, "failed because diplomacy was not employed to avert war but to make certain its coming." His chief "evidence" is that administration officials were aware that imposition of economic sanctions against Japan involved a risk that Japan would use force to obtain the raw materials it needed. This is certainly true, but it is a long distance from this to the statement that the administration imposed sanctions *because* the policy contained a risk of war. Morgenstern set out to prove more: that the Roosevelt administration made *certain* that war would result.

Perhaps one example of Morgenstern's interpretations will suffice to illustrate his extreme version of the isolationist thesis regarding the Roosevelt-Konoye meeting.

He writes that Hull's statement to Nomura that preliminary terms would be discussed with China, Britain, and the Netherlands "demonstrated unmistakably that this country already had an alliance, admitted or not, with China and the western imperialisms and was conducting its diplomacy much more with the view to protecting their interests than its own." Hull's actual purpose was to assure China, Britain, and the Netherlands that the United States would not betray to Japan their rights or territories. The American policy involved was anti-appeasement, which had been proclaimed time and again by Roosevelt and Hull as a policy designed primarily to serve the self-interest of the United States.[7] Incidentally Beard, although he approved Morgenstern's book, found in the documents reason to "put a stop to the vulgar saying: 'The United States was raking British chestnuts out of the fire.' "[8]

It cannot be admitted that with Konoye's fall the last chance of avoiding war with Japan disappeared. If the Roosevelt administration had been willing to support Japan's past and future program of aggression, the Tojo government would very likely have been happy to drop the plan to attack the United States, at least temporarily. The actions of Roosevelt and Hull lead one to assume that they believed the risk of new Japanese aggressions was preferable to a profoundly immoral Far Eastern Munich. History had proved that appeasement was not only immoral but also that aggressors could not be permanently appeased. The most that could have been accomplished by a Far Eastern Munich was to postpone a little longer new Japanese aggressions. This was no temptation for Roosevelt and Hull because it would be more than bal-

[5] *Ibid.*, 190, 496–506.
[6] JCC, *Report of the Joint Committee, Minority Report*, 497.

[7] Morgenstern, *Pearl Harbor*, 128, 139–40.
[8] Beard, *Roosevelt*, 504n.

anced by the degradation of the American and all free peoples, because it would violate the American commitment in the Lend Lease Act to aid peaceful nations against aggression, and because it was in any case politically impossible: the great majority of the American people long since had given up indifference to immorality in international relations. . . .

The Wrong Foot

Another grave accusation of the isolationists is that Roosevelt and Hull so conducted negotiations with Kurusu as to coerce the Japanese into attacking the United States. The assumption is made that if the United States refused to make an agreement with Japan, this amounted to coercion of the Japanese and created a situation in which not the Japanese but Roosevelt and Hull were responsible for the Japanese attack that followed. A necessary corollary of the argument is that Kurusu and the Tojo government did in fact "urgently desire" not merely *an* agreement with the United States but one that should have been accepted by Hull and Roosevelt. Charles A. Beard proves at great length that the Japanese did "urgently desire" *an* agreement, which was doubtless true. If the Tojo government could gain the objectives of its aggressive program with the cooperation of the United States, it is difficult to believe that sheer quixoticism would have led it to reject such an arrangement and risk defeat in war instead. Even this, however, it may be noted in passing, was the choice of Mussolini when France and Britain offered him his price if he would take it without war.

Beard finds in a Japanese proposal on November 20 for a "truce" or *"modus vivendi"* an opportunity for Hull, knowing that it was Japan's "last effort," that the American Army and Navy needed

time for preparations, and that a two-front war should "if humanly possible" be avoided, to use "supreme diplomatic ingenuity," and "supreme statesmanship" to "keep conversations going. . . ." Hull on November 26 rejected the Japanese proposal. In Beard's view, Hull "for reasons which are nowhere explicit" failed the supreme test of his career and answered the Japanese with what Beard calls "an ultimative notice."[9]

It is now possible to state certain facts of the situation which were not available to Beard. They suggest that he was too hasty in condemning Hull's statesmanship without sufficient data regarding the possibility that it was Japanese statesmanship, or lack of it, that was responsible for the failure of diplomacy and outbreak of war. After the war, the International Military Tribunal for the Far East found in the Japanese archives the story of Japanese purposes and plans. On November 5, an Imperial Conference decided that if the United States did not accept Japan's terms by November 25 (later extended to November 29), Japan would attack the United States. On November 10, the task force which had been organized and trained to bomb Pearl Harbor was ordered to the Kurile Islands and the date of December 7 was fixed for the attack. On November 22, the task force was ordered to proceed from the Kuriles to Hawaii. These actions were taken *before Hull answered Japan's "last offer" of November 20*. Foreign Minister Togo described the Japanese terms of November 20 as an "ultimatum."[10]

In short, Beard's mistake is that he puts the shoe on the wrong foot. Hull was incapable of issuing an "ultimative notice" to the Japanese after November 20 for the reason that Japan had already issued an

[9] *Ibid.*, 506–16.

[10] Ballantine, "Mukden to Pearl Harbor," 662–4.

ultimatum to the United States on that date, and proceeded to carry out its military threat within two days, before Hull answered its diplomatic threat. Beard would make the Roosevelt administration appear guilty of an aggression in diplomacy which he believes "explains," if it does not excuse, the subsequent Japanese aggression at Pearl Harbor. Actually it was Japan that was guilty of diplomatic as well as military aggression against the United States. Hull knew from Magic intercepts that the Japanese proposals of November 20 constituted an ultimatum involving demands, a deadline, and threat of attack. The only thing he did not know was that the attack was directed at Pearl Harbor or any American territory.

The Modus Vivendi

The Japanese on November 20 offered a draft proposal for a "temporary agreement." In the light of the rejection by the Japanese government, on November 19, of Nomura's suggestion in favor of such an agreement, this proposal must be regarded as the sheerest of hypocrisies designed to occupy the time while the Japanese task force proceeded to Hawaii. Two of the chief issues on which the United States desired settlement, namely, Japan's obligation under the Axis alliance, and economic policy in China and the Pacific regions, were left for later consideration. On remaining issues, Japan offered to make one concession, withdrawal of Japanese troops from southern to northern Indo-China, in return for United States cooperation with Japan in securing the fruits of aggression in China. Japan asked the United States to stop giving aid to China and to restore economic relations with Japan, including delivery to Japan of a required quantity of oil, while Japan made "peace" with China. Kurusu had admitted to Hull that

"peace" with China would involve the stationing of Japanese troops there for an indefinite period. Besides providing Japan with American oil to help it impose its will on China, the United States was asked to "cooperate" with Japan in obtaining for it oil and other materials in the NEI. Japan would promise to make no armed movement southward, but offered no guaranty against aggression northward.[11]

Hull considered that the proposals called for "virtually a surrender" by the United States. He asked Kurusu and Nomura, as he later wrote:

what they thought would be the public reaction in the United States if we were to announce tomorrow that we had decided to discontinue aid to Great Britain. There was no reply. "In the minds of the American people," I continued, "the purposes underlying our aid to China are the same as the purposes underlying aid to Great Britain. . . ."[12]

Hull regarded the situation as virtually hopeless. But the military leaders pleaded with him for more time, and therefore Hull and State Department officials sought desperately to work out some counterproposal to keep the conversations going. For a few days a three-months' *modus vivendi* was considered. It is noteworthy that it was while Hull worked on this scheme that the Japanese task force was ordered on November 22 to proceed eastward through the north Pacific to reach Hawaii by December 7. No inkling of this reached American observers or officials in Washington, but ominous movements of Japanese forces into positions where they were poised for attacks against Thailand, Malaya, the NEI, and possibly the Philippines or

[11] *Foreign Relations: Japan*, II, 748-9, 755-6.
[12] *Memoirs of Cordell Hull*, II, 1070-1.

Guam, were known in detail. On November 24, Army and Navy commanders in the Pacific were warned that a Japanese "surprise aggressive movement in any direction including an attack on the Philippines or Guam is a possibility."[13] This was interpreted in Hawaii to require no change in preparations against sabotage as the chief danger.

President Roosevelt, Secretary of the Treasury Morgenthau, and other officials helped Hull explore the possibility of a *modus vivendi,* and he consulted the representatives of Great Britain, China, the Netherlands, and Australia. A Magic intercept from Tokyo to Kurusu and Nomura on November 22 extended the deadline from November 25 to 29. One phrase in it provides the first reason why Hull in the end decided not to make a counterproposal for a *modus vivendi.* The Japanese Ambassadors were instructed: "Stick to our fixed policy. . . ." This could only mean that nothing but complete American surrender to the Japanese proposals would satisfy Tojo. It confirmed Hull's belief that no arrangement that the United States could accept would be acceptable to Japan. The intercepted message ended: "This time we mean it, that the deadline absolutely cannot be changed. After that things are automatically going to happen."[14]

The second reason why Hull decided against the *modus vivendi* is that the government of China objected to it and obtained wide support for its objection, including that of Churchill. The final American draft of the *modus vivendi* called for mutual pledges that the United States and Japan would not advance in the Pacific area by force or threat of force; Japan would withdraw its troops from

southern Indo-China, and also reduce its forces in northern Indo-China to 25,000 — a number thought to preclude a campaign to close the Burma Road; the United States would allow limited quantities of American oil, cotton, and other commodities to go to Japan and it would buy Japanese goods; the United States would urge Britain, Australia, and the Netherlands to resume trade similarly with Japan; and the United States affirmed its fundamental position that any settlement between Japan and China must be based upon the principles of "peace, law, order, and justice." Attached to this three-months' *modus vivendi* was a ten-point proposal for a permanent agreement.[15]

The *modus vivendi* drawn up by Hull meant temporary appeasement of Japan insofar as it would give temporary United States approval to Japanese conquests and relax the economic sanctions which the United States, Britain, Australia and the Netherlands had imposed against Japan during preceding months. The plan must be regarded as a product of the desperation of the Roosevelt administration in its fight for time. Had it been offered to Japan, it would have been a violation of the administration's principle of no compromise with aggression.

Only agreement by China, the government which would be the chief victim of this appeasement, that the time which might be gained would be worth the sacrifice, would have justified such an offer to Japan. China refused to agree. Churchill supported the Chinese view. After hectic discussions, the decision was reached on the night of November 25, to make no counterproposal of a *modus vivendi* but to answer the Japanese only with the ten-point proposal for a permanent settlement.[16]

[13] JCC, *Hearings,* Vol. 84, Pt. 14, Exhibit 37, p. 1405.
[14] *Memoirs of Cordell Hull,* II, 1074.

[15] *Ibid.,* 1072–3, 1077–81.
[16] *Ibid.,* 1074–81.

On the Rock of Principle

In this decision the Roosevelt administration met the supreme test of its statesmanship in service of the policy of collective security against aggression. Beard's statement that the decision was made "for reasons which are nowhere explicit"[17] is nonsense; Beard himself recites the evidence that the Chinese government violently opposed the *modus vivendi*. He ignores another contributing factor, that is, the futility of offering to Japan, in the face of the intercepted instructions to the Ambassadors to "stick to our fixed policy," an American *modus vivendi* which would have required Japan to retreat from its "fixed policy," especially in the matter of the number of troops to be left in northern Indo-China. Beard does not wish to admit that the one thing which might have justified temporary appeasement of Japan was the consent of China. The Roosevelt administration refused to make a deal with Japan affecting China's fate without its consent. It refused to ignore the rights of China as Chamberlain had ignored those of Czechoslovakia at Munich.

On the rock of this principle, the last possibility of Roosevelt and Hull attempting to postpone the deadline in Japan's ultimatum collapsed. Actually, no such possibility existed. But the administration believed that a possibility still existed that Japan would only attack non-American territory, leaving room for a choice by the United States whether it should enter the war.

No one but an absolute pacifist would argue that the danger of war is a greater evil than violation of principle. It must be concluded that the isolationist thesis involves denunciation of the Roosevelt-Hull decision against the *modus vivendi* because of the nature of the principle

[17] Beard, *Roosevelt*, 515.

involved. The isolationist believes that appeasement of Japan without China's consent violated no principle worth a risk of war. The internationalist must believe that the principle did justify a risk of war. In short, subjective and *a priori* attitudes ultimately determine judgment of the Roosevelt-Hull policy. If an observer can be imagined to exist who is "neutral" as between the attitudes of isolationists and internationalists, he might conclude that it did not matter whether or not the Roosevelt administration offered the *modus vivendi* because the Japanese government was certain to reject it.

A Third Choice?

By means of innuendos rather than overt statement, Beard implies that the Roosevelt administration had a third choice besides appeasement or refusal to appease, and took it: war. He combs the record to find "war-like" statements of the leaders in Washington, and presents them in sinister array entirely out of context. The President and his Cabinet on November 25, Beard writes, "discussed war, not prospects of peace. . . ." In Beard's vocabulary, discussion of war is synonymous with a desire for war. Secretary Stimson wrote in his diary regarding a meeting of the "War Council" with Roosevelt on November 25, which was attended by him and Hull, Knox, Marshall, and Stark, that Roosevelt brought up the likelihood that the Japanese, notorious for surprise attacks, would attack the United States within two days:

and the question was what we should do. The question was how we should maneuver them into the position of firing the first shot without allowing too much danger to ourselves. It was a difficult proposition.

Beard quotes this and Stimson's later

amplification to the Joint Congressional Committee:

In spite of the risk involved, however, in letting the Japanese fire the first shot, we realized that in order to have the full support of the American people it was desirable to make sure that the Japanese be the ones to do this so that there should remain no doubt in anyone's mind as to who were the aggressors.

These, and many variations of the theme in discussions in Washington, Beard assembles to suggest that the administration wanted war with Japan. He entitles his final chapter, dealing with the outbreak of war: "Maneuvering the Japanese into Firing the First Shot."[18]

The part of the Japanese government in maneuvering itself into firing the first shot is not discussed by Beard. The situation as he describes it leads a reader to believe that it was the United States that took the initiative for war during the weeks preceding December 7, while Japan was coerced into beginning a war it had sought to avoid. Stimson's word "maneuver" is magnified out of all relation to the actual position of the two governments in which Japan, of course, exercised the initiative and the United States was forced into a war it had sought to avoid. After creating suspicion in the reader's mind that Stimson and the other leaders knew that the Japanese intended to attack Pearl Harbor, and that they wanted the attack to occur, Beard makes Stimson's use of the word "maneuver" appear to have been an affirmation of the administration's knowledge and desire. But, as has been shown, the administration thought exclusively in terms of a Japanese movement southward. The question was whether the President should

ask Congress for a declaration of war *prior* to a Japanese attack on the Philippines or Guam, in order to avoid giving Japan the advantage of a surprise attack, or wait until Japan attacked United States territory, that is, "maneuver" Japan into firing the first shot. Despite much discussion, no final decision to ask Congress for a declaration of war was made. The other course, waiting while Japan might attack the United States, was a "maneuver" only in the sense that it involved avoidance of any action that would make the United States even *seem* to provoke or justify an attack by Japan. Whereas Beard makes the word appear to mean that the administration took positive actions to coerce the Japanese into attacking, it actually meant that the United States should do nothing that would give Japan an excuse for war.

The Southward Expedition

Beard calls the United States reply on November 26 to the Japanese proposal of November 20 an "ultimative notice." Morgenstern calls it more simply an "ultimatum."[19] The Minority Report of the Joint Congressional Committee declares that Japan "treated" the answer "as an ultimatum," and that Hull on November 28, if not on November 26, knew that it would so treat it.[20] Dramatic proof came on November 25 that it was Japan that had not only issued an ultimatum on November 20 but proceeded to carry out its new program of aggression without waiting for an answer from the United States. On the afternoon of the 25th, intelligence reports to Secretary Stimson stated that five Japanese divisions were moving southwards from Shantung and Shansi towards Indo-China or points be-

[18] *Ibid.*, 517–9 ff.

[19] Morgenstern, *Pearl Harbor*, 288 *et passim*.

[20] JCC, *Minority Report*, 563–4.

yond.[21] If more evidence were needed by the administration that the Japanese government had no intention of accepting any *modus vivendi* or any arrangement that would inhibit its program of conquest, this provided it. The President and Hull were sent copies of the report. Morgenstern avoids assessing this intelligence report at its face value by noting that on the next day, when Hull discussed with Stimson his decision to reject the *modus vivendi*, he "did not refer to the Japanese troop movement." Morgenstern notes that when the President on the 26th heard of the troop movement from Stimson, he said it "changed the whole situation, because it was an evidence of bad faith on the part of the Japanese. . . ." But, writes Morgenstern, the Hull answer to Japan that day had already "changed the whole situation."[22]

The United States was actually incapable of "changing the whole situation" no matter what it did short of an attack against Japan, and even this in the circumstances would have been an offensive action only on the level of tactics: Japan had already seized the initiative of the offensive on the higher level of strategy. The Japanese aggressive movement southward was obviously launched well before the Japanese government expected any reply to its proposal of a *modus vivendi*. News of it in Washington merely *confirmed* one of the premises upon which the decision was made to reject the *modus vivendi*: that Japan acted in bad faith. Beyond this, it is clear now that Japan was willing to expose its bad faith by moving an expedition southward in plain view because it served as a screen for its more stunning act of bad faith in sending the expedition to Pearl Harbor.

21 JCC, *Hearings*, Vol. 83, Pt. 11, pp. 5433–4.
22 Morgenstern, *Pearl Harbor*, 288.

Considering the scope of Japanese bad faith, what was hidden from Washington as well as what was exposed, one may call suspicion of Japan, which was the fundamental source of Chinese and all other opposition to the *modus vivendi*, the highest statesmanship. Had the *modus vivendi* been accepted, the lowering of guard and injury to morale among all anti-Axis peoples and governments would have invited disaster much more severe than actually occurred. Japan in its diplomacy and its military actions had already launched new aggressions against every Pacific power before the United States had an opportunity to accept or reject the *modus vivendi*. To search in such a situation for ignorance among Washington officials of the full scope of Japanese aggression in order to fix war guilt on them is ludicrous, especially in view of the charge by the same critics that Washington officials should have been more suspicious than they were of Japanese intentions at Pearl Harbor.

Even if Hull's November 26 answer to Japan had been an ultimatum, it would have been a nullity because Japan had issued one earlier and was acting on it. While it is conceivable that the orders to the Pearl Harbor expedition, and even the southward expedition, could have been rescinded during the days that remained prior to December 7, it is still true that the very act of sending those expeditions in the directions of their respective targets while "negotiations" proceeded in Washington constituted a threat of war signifying not merely bad faith but that those negotiations took place under the sanction of a Japanese ultimatum.

The Message of November 26

Hull's answer on November 26 was a refusal to surrender to the Japanese ultimatum. This was implicit in his rejection of the Japanese proposal for a *modus vivendi*. But he did not entirely reject that proposal, and he offered Japan a draft plan for an agreement on all points at issue as a basis for continued negotiations. This took away from his answer all character of a challenge to Japan to carry out its threat of war. Hull did not expect the Japanese government to accept his constructive proposal for an agreement, and he warned the armed service chiefs that Japan could be expected now to attack, but this was not, as the isolationists charge, proof that he regarded his answer as an "ultimatum." It was proof that he judged correctly that Japan would attack if the United States did not entirely surrender to Japan's ultimatum.

Hull's draft proposal for an American-Japanese agreement contained ten points. None of them was unacceptable or disadvantageous to a Japanese government mindful of the real interests of Japan: 1) a multilateral nonaggression pact among the governments principally concerned in the Pacific; 2) an agreement among the governments principally interested to respect the territorial integrity of Indo-China and equality of economic opportunity in that country; 3) no support of any Chinese government except the national government of Chiang Kai-shek; 4) relinquishment of extraterritorial rights in China by the United States as well as all other powers; 5) a liberal trade agreement between the United States and Japan; 6) mutual removal of freezing measures; 7) stabilization of currency values between the dollar and the yen; 8) an agreement that neither country would interpret an agreement with a third country in a way that would conflict with the fundamental purpose of establishing peace; 9) both governments would use their influence to lead other governments to accept and carry out the princi-

ples of this American-Japanese agreement; 10) Japan would withdraw its forces from China and Indo-China.

This draft proposal was accompanied by an explanation that the United States government regarded "some" but not all of the points in the Japanese *modus vivendi* of November 20 as in conflict with the fundamental principles to which each government had committed itself. The American draft proposal was not offered as the only terms of agreement the United States was willing to accept. Hull explained to Nomura and Kurusu that it was offered as *"one practical exemplification of a program which this Government envisages as something to be worked out during our further conversations."*[23]

To sum up: the American answer to Japan on November 26 did not reject *all* of the terms of Japan's proposed *modus vivendi;* the American draft proposal was not offered as the *only* terms of agreement the United States would accept; the United States made *no* demands upon Japan; the American draft proposal contained many offers that the Japanese had often admitted were advantageous to Japan because they would satisfy Japanese demands for security and prosperity — most significantly, an offer to end United States economic sanctions against Japan; it named *no deadline* for an answer by Japan; it contained *no threat of force or war* or other penalty if Japan refused to accept the American proposal; it specifically *invited* Japan to *continue negotiations;* it *promised to consider* new Japanese proposals, in the usual manner of a peaceful power, in the course of further negotiations.

To call such a proposal an "ultimatum" or an "ultimative notice" is to murder the

[23] *Foreign Relations: Japan,* II, 764–70. Italics added.

meaning of the word. If, as the Minority Report asserts, the Japanese war lords "treated" this answer "as an ultimatum," evidence is available, in Togo's description of the Japanese terms of November 20 as an ultimatum, which proves that he, at least, had for some days already accepted the fact which American isolationists reject: that to the Japanese government belonged the responsibility for war that accrues to a government guilty of issuing an ultimatum. When the Japanese Foreign Minister admits responsibility, it seems excessive for Americans to find the Japanese innocent and their own government guilty. . . .

Henry L. Stimson and McGeorge Bundy:
ON ACTIVE SERVICE

STIMSON had the highest respect for Franklin Roosevelt's political acumen, and at no time was he prepared to assert categorically that the President's method was wrong; all he could say was that it was emphatically not the method he himself would have chosen, and that in his opinion the President would have been an even greater politician if he had been a less artful one. This difference between the two men was basic to their natures. In this particular instance it will perhaps never be possible to say with certainty which was right; our task here is merely to present the issue as Stimson saw it.

The central point was stated to the President by Stimson in a private meeting on April 22. "I warned him in the beginning that I was going to speak very frankly and I hoped that he wouldn't feel that I did not have the real loyalty and affection for him that I did have. He reassured me on that point and then I went over the whole situation of the deterioration in the American political situation toward the war that has taken place since nothing happened immediately after the [Lend-Lease] victory. I cautioned him on the necessity of his taking the lead and that without a lead on his part it was useless to expect the people would vountarily take the initiative in letting him know whether or not they would follow him if he did take the lead." (Diary, April 22, 1941)

Stimson was certain that if the President were himself to go to the country and say frankly that force was needed and he wanted the country's approval in using it, he would be supported. In contrast to this policy, the President's method seemed to him to be one of cautious waiting for circumstance to get the fight started for him. The President was determined to avoid a setback at the hands of the isolationists, and he seriously feared that any overboldness on his part would lead to such a defeat.

On May 6 Stimson delivered a radio address, the text of which had been seen and passed by the President, expressing his own general view of the crisis, so far as loyalty to the President permitted. He

From *On Active Service in Peace and War* by Henry L. Stimson and McGeorge Bundy (New York: Harper and Brothers), pages 369–376. Copyright, 1948, by Henry L. Stimson.

came out flatly for active naval assistance to the British, pointing out that any other course would mean the annulment of the objectives of the Lend-Lease Act. And in the last two paragraphs he stated as clearly as he dared his conviction that war was coming.

. . . I am not one of those who think that the priceless freedom of our country can be saved without sacrifice. It can not. That has not been the way by which during millions of years humanity has slowly and painfully toiled upwards towards a better and more humane civilization. The men who suffered at Valley Forge and won at Yorktown gave more than money to the cause of freedom.

Today a small group of evil leaders have taught the young men of Germany that the freedom of other men and nations must be destroyed. Today those young men are ready to die for that perverted conviction. Unless we on our side are ready to sacrifice and, if need be, die for the conviction that the freedom of America must be saved, it will not be saved. Only by a readiness for the same sacrifices can that freedom be preserved.

There was no bitterness in Stimson's disagreement with the President. One day at a Cabinet meeting, "the President talked a little about his program of patrol and what he was planning to do, . . . and after narrating what had been done he said, 'Well, it's a step forward.' I at once said to him, 'Well, I hope you will keep on walking, Mr. President. Keep on walking.' The whole Cabinet burst into a roar of laughter which was joined in by the President." (Diary, April 25, 1941)

Although it was one of the strongest, along with a speech by Secretary Knox, Stimson's speech of May 6 was only one of many by administration leaders in this period. Stimson was interested to discover that he and Knox were not the only members of the Cabinet who were disturbed at the President's apparent fail-ure to follow up more rapidly his victory in the Lend-Lease Act. Jackson and Ickes were also worried. The President had his more cautious advisers, however, notably in the State Department. In Mr. Roose-velt's preparations for his own radio speech of May 27, he faced the contrast-ing advice of two camps, and although the final speech was much stronger than Stimson had feared it might be, it was not nearly so strong as he had hoped. The President firmly asserted the doctrine of the freedom of the seas, and made it clear that he intended to use "all additional measures necessary" to assure the deliv-ery of supplies to Great Britain. He also declared an "unlimited national emerg-ency," thus giving the administration somewhat broader powers in dealing with the crisis. But when, on the following day in his press conference, he allowed him-self to say that this bold and vigorous speech did not mean that he planned to institute convoys, Stimson was deeply discouraged. He had himself urged a very different course; in a letter of May 24 to the President he had suggested that the President ask Congress for power "to use naval, air, and military forces of the United States" in the Atlantic battle.

Throughout June Stimson's anxiety in-creased, and in the first few days of July it reached its climax. On July 2 he made his only wholly pessimistic diary entry in five years. The Nazi attack on Russia had begun and was going altogether too well; meanwhile America seemed to have lost her way. "Altogether, tonight I feel more up against it than ever before. It is a prob-lem whether this country has it in itself to meet such an emergency. Whether we are really powerful enough and sincere enough and devoted enough to meet the Germans is getting to be more and more of a real problem." (Diary, July 2, 1941)

The next day he wrote the following

letter and memorandum to the President, who at the time was considering his message to Congress on the occupation of Iceland:

July 3, 1941

My dear Mr. President:

My thoughts are deeply with you during these critical days. When the time comes for you to speak, my view is that you should speak to the Congress not by message but face to face and do it with personal and disarming frankness. You are such a master of such intercourse that I hesitate even to suggest the points that you should cover.

The main thing it seems to me is to point out how you have done your best to serve the cause of peace and how events have proved too strong for you. That in my opinion is the most appealing and persuasive line and the one which will produce the following of the whole nation. It is the course which all of your constituents have themselves been obliged to follow.

I enclose merely a memorandum of some of the points to be covered, making no attempt at phraseology.

Faithfully yours,

Henry L. Stimson

The President,
Hyde Park, New York

MEMORANDUM FOR ADDRESS TO CONGRESS

I have sincerely hoped that we should not be drawn into this war. I have earnestly tried to avoid the use of force. I have labored with all my strength to secure a national defense, both naval and military, for this nation which would be sufficient to protect it when fighting alone against any combination of nations that might attack it. But my hope is becoming dim. The effort to avoid the use of force is proving ineffective. Our national defense is as yet far from complete. It has now become abundantly clear that, unless we add our every effort, physical and spiritual as well as material, to the efforts of those free nations who are still fighting for freedom in this world, we shall ourselves be brought to a situation where we shall be fighting alone at an enormously greater danger than we should encounter today with their aid.

The attitude suggested in this memorandum was rejected by the President, although the advice of such men as Stimson and Hopkins was again effective in offsetting more cautious counsel from other sources. In a meeting at the White House on July 6, Stimson told the President's advisers that "the President must be frank. Whether or not he was going to ask the Congress for action, he must in any event tell them exactly what he is doing and what he intends to do." (Diary, July 6, 1941) The President's message of July 7 did at least frankly state that he had moved American forces into Iceland and proposed to defend the sea communications between the United States and that island. In comparison with Stimson's own long draft, prepared on July 5 at Mr. Roosevelt's request, the President's message lacked emphasis on the central and controlling fact that Iceland was important principally as a way station on the North Atlantic route from America to Great Britain. It also omitted any intimation of war as imminent. The President was still content to build his case mainly on the defense of the Western Hemisphere, believing that this was a more palatable argument to the people, and one less subject to violent attack from the isolationists.

This effort in July was Stimson's last active attempt to bring the President to his way of thinking. It was clear that Mr. Roosevelt did not agree with him, and Stimson was inclined to believe after July that the President was so far committed to his own more gradual course that nothing could change him.

Moreover, as the summer wore on, the kind of lifting leadership which Stimson desired became less possible. "The chance for a trumpet call for a battle to save freedom throughout the world had been sunk in a quibble over the extent of defense and the limits of the Western Hemisphere." Meanwhile, what words might have accomplished earlier was being achieved by events; one of our patrolling destroyers was attacked, and the President publicly announced that the fleet would shoot on sight Axis vessels in the western Atlantic. While the President accomplished his object of having the war come to him, it should be observed that by this policy he in effect surrendered the initiative to the Nazis. By waiting for Nazi attacks on American vessels the President left it to them to choose their time to fight.

Looking back on this period Stimson could not avoid a comparison between Franklin Roosevelt and his distinguished cousin Theodore. From what he knew of both men, he was forced to believe that in the crisis of 1941 T.R. would have done a better and more clean-cut job than was actually done. Equally with his cousin he would have appreciated the true meaning of the Nazi threat, and there can be no higher praise, for no statesman in the world saw and described the Nazi menace more truly than Franklin Roosevelt. T.R.'s advantage would have been in his natural boldness, his firm conviction that where he led, men would follow. He would, Stimson felt sure, have been able to brush aside the contemptible little group of men who wailed of "war-

mongers," and in the blunt strokes of a poster painter he would have demonstrated the duty of Americans in a world issue. Franklin Roosevelt was not made that way. With unequaled political skill he could pave the way for any given specific step, but in so doing he was likely to tie his own hands for the future, using honeyed and consoling words that would return to plague him later.

The frame of mind of the American people under this treatment was graphically shown in a Gallup Poll at the end of April, 1941. To three questions the public gave three remarkable answers. Of those expressing an opinion, (1) nearly three-fourths would favor entering the war "if it appeared certain that there was no other way to defeat Germany and Italy," (2) four-fifths thought the United States would sooner or later enter the war, (3) four-fifths were opposed to immediate entry into the war.

The most striking fact about this result was that in the considered view of the leaders of the American Government, and also by facts publicly known, it was already clear that "there was no other way to defeat Germany and Italy" than by American entry into the war. The trouble was that no one in authority had said so.

In Stimson's view these answers exactly reflected the leadership of the President. The first answer showed how far he and others had succeeded in giving the American people a clear understanding of the fascist danger. The second answer reflected a somewhat fatalistic expectation that just as America had participated in every general European conflict for over two hundred years, she would probably get into this one too. The third answer, showing opposition to immediate entry, was the direct result of the fact that no responsible leader, and particularly not the President, had explicitly stated that

that was necessary; on the contrary, the President in particular had repeatedly said that it was *not* necessary.

To Stimson it always seemed that the President directed his arguments altogether too much toward his vocal but small isolationist opposition, and not toward the people as a whole. By his continuous assertion that war was *not* a likely result of his policy, he permitted the American people to think themselves into a self-contradictory frame of mind. As Stimson constantly pointed out at the time, only the President could take the lead in a warlike policy. Only he had the right and duty to lead his people in this issue.

If Mr. Roosevelt had been himself a believer in neutrality, as McKinley had been in 1898 or Wilson for so long in 1916, it would have been natural that effective pressure for action should develop in private places. But as the proclaimed and acknowledged champion of the anti-Axis cause, he was necessarily its spearhead in policy, and without word from him the American people could not be expected to consider all-out action necessary.

There are those who will maintain that this explanation of Stimson's feelings merely confirms their view that Franklin Roosevelt dishonestly pulled the American people into a war they never should have fought. Nothing could be farther from Stimson's own position, and it should be emphasized that if this charge is to be leveled against Mr. Roosevelt, it must in some degree be leveled at Stim-

son too. For the difference of policy between him and the President was one of degree, not of kind. Stimson saw war coming in December, 1940; it was not until April, 1941, that he began to feel that the President could successfully preach war to the people — there are always times, in politics, when it is impossible to speak with entire frankness about the future, as all but the most self-righteous will admit. *The essential difference between Stimson and the President was in the value they set on candor as a political weapon.* And as Stimson himself fully recognized, it was a good deal easier to advocate his policy, as Secretary of War, than to carry it out, as President. Certainly the consequences of failure in a bold course would have been extremely serious — no one can say whether the United States could have surmounted the reaction in feeling which would have set in if any proposal by the President had been roundly beaten in Congress or thoroughly disapproved by the people. On the other hand, it was equally true that the impasse into which America had thought herself in 1941 might have continued indefinitely if that had been the will of the Axis, and if this had happened, the President would have had to shoulder a large share of the blame. It did not happen, and all that America lost by her failure to enter the war earlier was time. But time in war means treasure and lives, and through the summer of 1941 Stimson was constantly faced with concrete examples of the losses incurred by delay....

Cordell Hull: THE MEMOIRS OF CORDELL HULL

WE had had two objectives in mind in all our relations with Japan since the outbreak of war in Europe, and especially since the fall of France. One was peace. The other, if peace could not be had, was to gain time to ready our defenses.

We failed to win peace, but we gained invaluable time.

It was not until twenty-seven months after the invasion of Poland, not until eighteen months after the fall of France, that Japan struck. Although we still needed more time to complete our defenses, nevertheless we were comparatively far better prepared on December 7, 1941, than we had been on September 1, 1939, or on June 17, 1940.

Prime Minister Churchill put it ably in his speech on December 26, 1941, to a joint session of Congress in Washington, by saying: "We have, indeed, to be thankful that so much time has been granted to us. If Germany had tried to invade the British Isles after the French collapse in June, 1940, and if Japan had declared war on the British Empire and the United States at about the same date, no one can say what disaster and agonies might not have been our lot. But now, at the end of December, 1941, our transformation from easy-going peace to total war efficiency has made very great progress."

Throughout all this period we had been firm in our dealings with Japan, though we were careful not to push her toward war; at the same time we always made it clear that we could and should live at peace in the Pacific.

We wanted peace with Japan for the sake of the better development of the world and also because we needed it. I felt that peace in the Pacific was necessary if we were to make an adequate contribution to the defense of Britain and the defeat of Hitler which was vital to our own security. Events in the Far East seemed of double importance to me because they were so closely interlocked with events in Europe. If at any time after France fell, Japan, with surface and underwater warships, had cut Britain's line of supplies and reenforcements from Australia, New Zealand, India, and South Africa, it is doubtful that the United Kingdom could have survived. Virtually alone we should then have faced Germany in the Atlantic and Japan in the Pacific.

When I entered into conversations with the Japanese in April, 1941, I determined to do everything I could to bring about a peaceful and fair settlement of the situation in the Pacific. Even though I realized at the very outset that the chances for such an agreement were no bigger than a gnat, I still felt we had to make the effort. Not only was such effort in accordance with the traditional attitude of the United States, but it was also imperative for our over-all concept of world defense against Hitlerism.

In the negotiations from April to December I was forever conscious of the stupendous responsibilities that devolved upon me. A series of momentous decisions had to be made, and in many cases the initiative had to come from me. I am very happy that the President and I worked throughout in perfect harmony to avoid any misstep in our discussions with Japan.

In those discussions there were involved issues decisive for our national honor and destiny. The decisions that had to be made placed upon the President and me a responsibility almost unthinkable in its breadth and depth. We had to decide whether to enter into discussions with Japan in the first place on the basis of her proposals of May 12; whether to break off negotiations in July, after Japan invaded Indo-China; whether to apply freezing restrictions to Japan; and whether to agree to a meeting between the President and Premier Konoye. We had to make a fateful decision as to how to deal with Japan's ultimatum of November 20, and whether to present a modus vivendi.

I had the task of conducting almost all the discussions with the Japanese Ambassadors and of suggesting to the President in advance what he might say to the Japanese in the conferences in which he took part. I had to assume the responsibility of concluding that the diplomatic phase of the negotiations was finished and of stating that the task of safeguarding the nation had passed into the hands of the Army and the Navy.

I never had any thought that Japan was bluffing. Instead, I was convinced she had embarked on a steady, fixed course of conquest that would reach us in her own chosen time. I believed she was playing the role of an international desperado, and it is the business of a desperado — whether a nation or an individual — to fight.

During the period of our conversations Japan believed she was exceedingly well armed to achieve her intended conquests in the Pacific. She likewise knew we were by no means sufficiently armed to resist her attack successfully. Therefore, when Japan presented her successive and ever harsher demands, I was satisfied she was not bluffing but rather was giving us a last chance to yield our basic principles and thus enable her to continue her conquests without further risk of serious resistance.

Premier Konoye's memoirs confirm this view. He relates that on September 6, 1941, an Imperial Conference was held at which "the basic principles for the carrying out of the national policy of the Empire" were determined. Several "basic principles" were these:

(1) The Empire shall perfect war preparations generally by the latter part of October with a determination to be prepared for war with America, England, and The Netherlands in order to assure its independent national existence and self-defense.

(2) Parallel with the foregoing, diplomatic measures vis-a-vis the United States and Great Britain shall be exhausted toward obtaining fulfillment of our demands. . . .

(3) In case there is no expectation of achievement of our demands by the aforesaid diplomatic measures within the first ten days of October, decision shall be made to go to war with the United States, Great Britain, and The Netherlands; policies other than those toward the southern regions shall be carried out in accordance with the already fixed decisions of the Government; and efforts shall be made to prevent a joint American-Soviet front against Japan from materializing.

Here was a cold-blooded determination to go to war — one of the most sinister episodes in history.

Japan's willingness to make war, plus the far greater state of her military preparedness, provides full explanation for our holding off as long as we did on applying embargoes on the shipment of petroleum, scrap iron, and other strategic materials to Japan. The President and I saw eye to eye on this policy. We felt that Japan might well retaliate in a military way if we cut off such shipments. Even if she did not attack us directly she might invade other areas, such as the Dutch East Indies, to obtain the products we denied her.

Prior to January, 1940, we had a commercial treaty with Japan, as with most all other countries, which obligated us to trade alike with each nation. Moreover, a strong segment of the American people stood adamantly for isolation and subjected any intimation of such a move as an embargo to a terrific bombardment of criticism. We could not but recall our failure in 1936 to induce Congress to enact a law that would have authorized us to impose embargoes on merely the export of materials above a normal peacetime level. This would have given legal effect to the moral embargo the President and I had instituted after the outbreak of the Italo-Ethiopian War. We could not but remember the fierce reaction to the President's "quarantine speech," one implication of which would have been the severance of commercial relations with Japan. We were assailed by other, contradictory critics, some even voicing violent threats, who one day shouted "Warmonger" if we made any suggestion to increase our military strength, and the next day demanded rigid embargoes against Japan. I often stated in reply that I did not believe in making a threat unless the nation was prepared to back up the Government; that if the Navy could accompany our policy in the Far East we would have no hesitation in embargoing Japan in any manner or at any time. But any half-informed person should have known that our Navy during those years of armament by the aggressor nations was not satisfactorily prepared to station itself for any time in the Far Eastern waters.

Furthermore, at the very intimation that the Navy would be sent to the other side of the earth to back up what we knew was a threat that might lead to dangerous complications with Japan, a large section of the American public would have almost crucified the Government officials advocating such a policy.

The British and Dutch Governments saw the possibility of Japanese military reaction to embargoes as well as we. During the negotiations between Japan and the Netherlands East Indies, from September, 1940, until June, 1941, the British and Netherlands Governments urged that we refrain from taking drastic steps to curtail exports to Japan because they feared that such curtailment might result in an increase of Japanese pressure and enlarged demands for concessions from the Netherlands Indies.

The President said publicly on July 24, 1941, that it was very essential from our own selfish point of view of defense to prevent a war from starting in the South Pacific, and that such a conflict might have resulted from our embargoing exports of petroleum to Japan. We had already begun, in October, 1940, to refuse all licenses for shipment of iron and steel scrap of any kind to Japan, after having already placed restrictions on the export of numerous basic materials. After our freezing of Japanese credits in July, 1941, trade with Japan virtually ceased. We had adopted restrictions on the export of strategic materials to Japan as rapidly as we felt would be prudent, and by proceeding in this way we gained the time we needed so desperately.

It is my considered opinion that, if Japan had attacked us six months before Pearl Harbor, the whole aspect of the world war might have changed. In that event Hitler most likely would have promptly abandoned his plan to attack

Russia. Feeling that Japan would tie the United States down in the Pacific and would cut off Britain from the assistance of Australia, New Zealand, India, and possibly South Africa, he might well have concentrated on the reduction of the United Kingdom by air and submarine warfare, and possibly invasion, leaving Russia to be dealt with later.

There were three methods to meet the danger from Japan. One was by a preventive attack. But democracies do not engage in preventive attacks except with greatest difficulty. Had I suggested to the President that he go to Congress and ask for a declaration of war against Japan at some time after the invasion of southern Indo-China, he could have made a good case concerning the dangers to us inherent in Japan's course of aggression. But, remembering the fact that on August 13, 1941, only three weeks after Japan invaded southern Indo-China, the House of Representatives sustained the Selective Service Act by a majority of just one vote, it seems most unlikely that the President could have obtained a declaration.

Nor would the military and naval authorities have been ready for a preventive attack. The fact that they pleaded for more time solely to prepare our defenses in the Pacific was proof in itself that they were not prepared to take the offensive.

A preventive attack, moreover, would have run counter to our determination to pursue the course of peace to the end, with the hope, however microscopic, that even at the last hour the Japanese might have a change of heart.

The second method to meet the danger was to agree to Japan's demands. This would have given us peace — that is, until Japan, after strengthening herself through the concessions we should have made, was ready to move again. But it would have denied all the principles of right living among nations which we had supported; it would have betrayed the countries that later became our allies; and it would have given us an infamous place in history.

When we realize that Japan was ruthlessly invading peaceful countries, that the United States had pleaded with her from the beginning to cease her course of military conquest in partnership with Hitler, and that all problems in the Pacific would have practically settled themselves if Japan had adopted a policy of peace, it is evident that Japan had no right to make demands upon us. Japan negotiated as if we, too, were an aggressor, as if both countries had to balance their aggressions. Japan had no more right to make demands upon us than an individual gangster has to make demands upon his intended victim.

The third method was simply to continue discussions with Japan, to convince her that her aggressions cost her more than they were worth, to point out to her that her partnership with Hitler could be as dangerous to her as it was to the rest of the world, to lay before her proposal after proposal which in the long run would have given her in peace the prosperity her military leaders were seeking in conquest.

It was this third that we chose. Of the three, it was the only American method.

Suggestions for Additional Reading

No American historian has yet tabulated the books and articles dealing with foreign affairs, the debates in the *Congressional Record,* or the discussions in public forums and over the radio by which the impact on the American people might be measured as war clouds gathered over Europe and Asia in the decade before the Japanese struck at Pearl Harbor. But from the outbreak of war in Europe in 1939, and particularly after the *Blitzkrieg* of the spring of 1940, a "Great Debate" engaged Congress, the press, and the public over the extent to which the United States should concern herself with affairs elsewhere in the world. The student will not find any sizable collection of the arguments of "isolationists" and "interventionists" gathered together, but must search for them in the press and the *Congressional Record.*

The surprise attack put a momentary stop to the debate, but it was almost immediately perceived that the issue of who was to blame for the disaster at Pearl Harbor implied judgments about Roosevelt's whole foreign policy in the years before war came. Both those supporting the administration and those who questioned its policy set on foot investigations to establish the facts. The requirements of wartime security prevented many of the details from becoming public during the first years of the war, but eventually a great mass of testimony was made available in the forty-odd volumes of the *Report* of the Joint Congressional Committee on Pearl Harbor, including both the majority and minority reports.

To the scant material available at first have been gradually added the diaries and memoirs of those concerned with America's foreign relations in the years before the war. Some archives have been opened, and the records of enemy countries have become available, from which historians in generous number have developed their interpretations of what happened. The student in search of facts or opinions concerning Roosevelt's foreign policy will find no dearth of material.

The selections included in the foregoing reading are centered for the most part directly on the main issues of the relations between the United States and Japan. Further reading in the books from which selections have been taken is recommended for a clear view of the whole problem of the coming of the war, since limitations of space made it necessary to omit much pertinent detail in the arguments of the authors.

To these may be added a number of other useful works. One of the best of the early efforts to acquaint the reader with the developments which led to war was *How War Came* (New York, 1942) by Forrest Davis and Ernest K. Lindley, two able journalists. Written before all the facts were in, it nevertheless reflects the views of perceptive observers of the Washington scene generally favorable to the Administration. Walter Millis in *This Is Pearl* (New York, 1947), has woven a highly readable account of the fateful and inexorable movement of events down to December 7, which leaves most of the blame for the disaster at Pearl Harbor resting on the commanders there. Another work centered on the limited subject of culpability for the military and naval defeat is the article by General Sherman Miles, in 1941 the Assistant Chief of Staff for Intelligence, "Pearl Harbor in Retrospect," *Atlantic Monthly*, July, 1948, which places responsibility squarely on General Short and Admiral Kimmel. In his volume on the history of the Navy in World War II, *Rising Sun in the Pacific*, Samuel Eliot Morison devotes the opening chapters to an analysis of Japanese policy in the Far East, attempting a balanced assessment of the factors in the surprise at Pearl Harbor, seeking to understand them rather than to apportion blame.

Turning to the more general discussions of the administration of American foreign policy, the point of view favorable to Roosevelt found in the selections from Feis and Rauch is supplemented by John Gunther's *Roosevelt in Retrospect* (New York, 1950), a readable but superficial account. The most substantial work to date is the thorough examination of policy undertaken by William L. Langer and S. Everett Gleason, *The Challenge to Isolation, 1937–1940*, the first of several volumes to come. Langer and Gleason conclude that Roosevelt and Hull did not desire to lead the United States into war and that their actions were nicely calculated to avoid involvement. These authors hold that Roosevelt lagged behind public opinion in moving toward participation in the world conflict, although their evidence furnishes some ground for the argument that the administration of foreign policy was often carelessly handled.

On the other side, in addition to the selections from Chamberlin, Tansill, and Beard in this volume, the case against Roosevelt and his advisers is argued emphatically in George Morgenstern, *Pearl Harbor: The Story of the Secret War* (New York, 1947). Morgenstern charges Roosevelt with secretly maneuvering a reluctant America into an unnecessary war by means of devious and unconstitutional methods. The result, the surprise attack on Pearl Harbor, was foreseeable and avoidable, he maintains, and he offers a refutation of the thesis that the field commanders were responsible for the disaster. He finds Roosevelt guilty of using that dramatic event to turn attention away from close scrutiny of the policies employed in the years before war came. Frederick C. Sanborn, a specialist in international law, subjects each of the Administration's moves to close examination, testing what was said with what was done, in his *Design for War: A Study of Secret Power Politics* (New York, 1951). He, too, believes that the American people were betrayed by illegal and undemocratic procedures perpetrated by the government, as does John T. Flynn, *The Roosevelt Myth* (New York, 1948), and both contend that Roosevelt sought war to save his political position.

The student may well want to read six lively articles which support or attack some of the above-mentioned books. One, by Samuel Eliot Morison, is a critical review of Beard's work, "Did Roosevelt Start the War — History through a Beard," *Atlantic Monthly*, August, 1948. Another, also highly critical of the revisionists, is Arthur M. Schlesinger, Jr., "Roosevelt and His Detractors," *Harper's Magazine*, June, 1950. The other four are available in pamphlet form from the Henry Regnery Company, Chicago, written by Harry Elmer Barnes in support of the revisionist writings of Beard, Morgenstern, Sanborn, Tansill, and Chamberlin. In *The Struggle against the Historical Blackout* (ninth revised, enlarged edition, no date), Barnes charges most American historians, publishers, and government authorities with lack of objectivity in viewing the problem of America's entry into war. He includes a critical review of Millis's book and highly favorable notice of Chamberlin and Sanborn. He attacks the reception given by book reviewers to works unfavorable to Roosevelt. In Barnes's eyes, the United States is slipping into the pattern portrayed in George Orwell's *Nineteen Eighty-Four*. His pamphlet *Was Roosevelt Pushed into War by Popular Demand in 1941?* enters a caveat against a paper read by Professor Dexter Perkins at the 1950 meeting of the American Historical Association which attempted to show by a survey of public opinion polls that the American people were behind the Administration's measures. Barnes's pamphlet *Rauch on Roosevelt* vigorously attacks Rauch's interpretations and impugns Rauch as an historian. *The Court Historians versus Revisionism* bitterly assails the volume by Langer and Gleason and promises a forthcoming revisionists' "symposium" which will add to the argument.

Two works which furnish important background on our Far Eastern relations and have important implications for an over-all judgment of our foreign policy past and present are A. Whitney Griswold's work, *The Far Eastern Policy of the United States* (New York, 1938), and George F. Kennan's *American Diplomacy 1900–1950*. These two works are supplemented by an article bearing directly on our relations with Japan written by Joseph W. Ballantine, who worked at the side of Cordell Hull during the difficult negotiations before the war: "Mukden to Pearl Harbor," *Foreign Affairs,* July, 1949.

Equipped with the knowledge of events and with the arguments before him, the reader may want to explore the writings of some of the actors in the drama and judge their motives for himself. In addition to further profitable reading in the memoirs of Stimson and Hull, from which selections have been taken, much of value may be found in Robert E. Sherwood's *Roosevelt and Hopkins* (New York, 1948). Sherwood was close to both men, and has drawn heavily from records they left. Other pertinent works are Joseph C. Grew's *Ten Years in Japan* (New York, 1944) and the account by a Japanese liberal, Toshikazu Kase, *Journey to the Missouri* (New Haven, 1950). *The Public Papers and Addresses of Franklin Delano Roosevelt*, edited by Judge Samuel I. Rosenman, contain, in Volume X, much material of value for the problem. The viewpoint of the British government is provided in Volume 3 of Winston S. Churchill's account of the war, entitled *The Grand Alliance* (Boston, 1950). A convenient collection of documents and speeches in connection with the issue is *The Record of American Diplomacy*, edited by Ruhl J. Bartlett (New York, 1947), pages 564–636.